Published in conjunction with the exhibition
of the same name, held from 20 September 1997
to 11 January 1998 in the Frank L. Horton Museum Center at
Old Salem, Winston-Salem, North Carolina.

Library of Congress Cataloging-in-Publication Data
Locklair, Paula W., 1950–
Quilts, coverlets, and counterpanes: bedcoverings from the
MESDA and Old Salem collections / Paula W. Locklair.
p. cm.
Catalog of an exhibition held from September 20, 1997
to January 11, 1998 in the Frank L. Horton Museum Center
at Old Salem, Winston-Salem, N.C.
Includes bibliographic references.
ISBN 1-879704-04-8 (alk. paper)
1. Quilts—Southern States—History—18th century—Exhibitions.
2. Quilts—Southern States—History—19th century—Exhibitions.
3. Quilts—North Carolina—Winston-Salem—Exhibitions.
4. Coverlets—Southern States—History—18th century—
Exhibitions. 5. Coverlets—Southern States—History—
19th century—Exhibitions. 6. Coverlets—North Carolina—
Winston-Salem—Exhibitions. 7. Museum of Early Southern
Decorative Arts—Exhibitions. 8. Old Salem, Inc.—Exhibitions.
I. Museum of Early Southern Decorative Arts.
II. Old Salem, Inc. III. Title.
NK9112.L63 1997
746.46'0975'07475667—dc21   97-18406
                                              CIP

Distributed by The University of North Carolina Press,
P.O. Box 2288, Chapel Hill, North Carolina 27515-2288

Photography by Wesley Stewart unless otherwise noted.

Editorial and production: Cornelia B. Wright

Design: Catherine Horne, M&Company

Printed and bound by Everbest Printing Co., Hong Kong

Preface

Bedcoverings, as an integral part of the material culture of the South, have been collected and catalogued by Old Salem and the Museum of Early Southern Decorative Arts (MESDA) as part of their ongoing efforts to represent how people in the past lived. With the new changing exhibits space provided by the Frank L. Horton Museum Center at Old Salem, we have the opportunity to present some of the highlights of our own textile collection in an exhibition. This is also the first time that most of these pieces have been published and that they have been considered in relationship to the documentary material available.

The contributions of Old Salem and MESDA to this exhibition are distinctive and complementary. Since the early 1970s, MESDA, a division of Old Salem, has collected documentary and photographic information about artisans and culture from the seventeenth century through 1820 for the states of Maryland, Virginia, Kentucky, Tennessee, North and South Carolina, and Georgia. The MESDA Index of Artisans database contains a wealth of information about textiles and bedding, information gleaned from newspapers, court records, wills, inventories, and personal papers from these states. All period references come from this resource unless otherwise noted. The bedcoverings collected by MESDA span the late eighteenth to the mid-nineteenth century. Old Salem's collections represent bedcoverings made and used in the Moravian town of Salem in the nineteenth century, documented in turn by family histories and by the extensive records kept by the Moravian church. Salem's collection also includes a number of needleworking

tools and implements that offer insight into the methods used to create the masterpieces presented here, and the pride of workmanship that adorned even these utilitarian objects. The Wachovia Historical Society collection also provided some quilts with a Salem provenance.

The selection of bedcoverings was based on provenance, condition, and type. Nearly all of the pieces in the exhibition are from the South. Only five are simply "American" with no specific provenance, but intrinsic in each of them are important stylistic features which contribute to our understanding of early bedcoverings. For nineteen of the bedcovers we have the name of the maker, and another has the maker's initials, but the full name is unknown.

I am indebted to many colleagues for their assistance. For content development and object selection, I thank Sally Gant, Carol Hall, Becky Minnix, Margaret Shearin, and Margaret Vincent; for general support and preparation of the bedcoverings for photography, I am grateful to my assistants Johanna Brown and Michelle Fulp. The manuscript was reviewed by John Larson, Brad Rauschenberg, Carol Hall, and Margaret Vincent; their insights were consistently helpful. I am especially appreciative of the guidance given by Colleen Callahan, curator of costumes and textiles at the Valentine Museum, who carefully read and critiqued the manuscript in its early form.

PAULA W. LOCKLAIR
Director of Collections and Curator,
Old Salem & MESDA

Introduction

The title *Quilts, Coverlets & Counterpanes* uses terms that for centuries have described the outer coverings used on beds. In period records such as estate inventories, wills, and newspaper advertisements, these terms were used in various combinations and in some cases seemingly interchangeably. However, it is clear that the people recording them saw distinctions between the terms, even though they may have been subtle, and that these distinctions changed over time. Because the descriptions are often not detailed, from our twentieth-century perspective it is usually difficult to know what seventeenth-, eighteenth-, or nineteenth-century writers were calling a "quilt," "coverlet," or "counterpane." This confusion over terminology continues today.

For the purposes of this exhibition, a *quilt* is a bedcovering having a top and back, and perhaps a filler of cotton or wool, that have been quilted together, usually with a running stitch in a pattern. A *counterpane* is a bedcovering of only one layer that has been decorated by embroidery. A *coverlet* is probably the most difficult to isolate in meaning because historically it has been used almost as a generic term for a bedcovering. It will be used here both in that way and as a descriptive term for the woven overshot "coverlets" of the nineteenth century.

Styles and techniques used in early bedcoverings

The bedcoverings in this exhibition are a representative sampling from the MESDA and Old Salem

Fig. 1. Detail of cut-chintz appliqué with decorative embroidery, cat. 22.

collections. They illustrate four primary types that were both useful and decorative: embroidered, patchwork, appliquéd, and woven.

For the most part, the patchwork and appliquéd designs in these bedcovers are similar to those used by quilt makers throughout the United States and Canada in the late eighteenth and early nineteenth centuries. Because many of the quilts in this exhibition are signed, dated, or accompanied by documented family histories, these particular designs can be substantiated as being known and used in the South.

The album quilt, which has a Baltimore heritage, is one of the few configurations that can be called southern; examples of this style are the quilts shown as cat. 24, 27, and 28. All of these share the characteristics of bold, clear, and whimsical designs cut from colorful fabrics, predominately red and green printed cotton calico, applied to a white cotton ground with tiny stitches. Cat. 24 also has faded examples of the rainbow-printed fabrics that were very popular on Baltimore album quilts.

The central diamond medallion style (cat. 21 and 22), while not unique to the South, seems to have had a special appeal to southern quilt makers, especially in North Carolina and Virginia. Quilts with this motif can have a combination of woodblock, copperplate, and roller-printed fabrics. The appliqués were often sewn to the top with a decorative stitch, such as a reverse buttonhole stitch, in silk thread. This served to keep the appliqué from unrav-

5

eling, as the edges were often not turned under, and it also was a decorative element in itself. Sometimes portions of the appliqués were embroidered in the same silk thread to give definition and to highlight elements of the print (fig. 1).

The all-white bedcoverings presented here are a lasting legacy of the high degree of embroidery skill of their makers. Each white counterpane or quilt generally uses predominantly one type of decorative embroidery, such as tufted candlewicking, stuffed and corded work, or a smoother embroidery technique such as a satin stitch; the first two give a three-dimensional quality, while the last produces a more subtle effect. Because these pieces are white-on-white, their success depends on the maker's ability to create sufficient light-and-shadow contrast through the design and choice of embroidery stitches and techniques. A superior example of the embroiderer as artist is cat. 2 (fig. 2), a counterpane by Amelia Nash of Kentucky, which exhibits great skill not only in its embroidery and intricate openwork, but also in the inspired balance and flow of its asymmetrical design.

The earliest dated bedcover in the exhibition (cat. 1), from 1793, is in this category of white embroidered bedcoverings. It is also the exhibition's earliest southern example of the central medallion design, which in the eighteenth century was popular in patchwork quilts (cat. 31) as well as in embroidery and whole-cloth quilting patterns (cat. 9), and in the nineteenth century was interpreted in patch-

Fig. 2. Detail of openwork embroidery, cat. 2.

work and appliqué (cat. 19 and 25).

Related to the all-white pieces are two signed and dated counterpanes (cat. 6 and 7) from South Carolina. Like the all-white examples, the ground is white; the difference is that the embroidery in both is in shades of red and blue, with some white added in cat. 6, allowing the embroiderer to rely more on color and design than on her skill with a needle to provide the overall effect. Even though both of these counterpanes have a central medallion, the earlier piece (cat. 6) exhibits a certain naiveté in the use of out-of-scale bugs and butterflies scattered among flowers and swags (fig. 3). The later example (cat. 7), from 1823, is a balanced and somewhat restrained, yet elegant, composition.

The primary purpose of woven coverlets, in contrast to the appliquéd, patchwork, and embroidered bedcoverings, was warmth. As is the case with quilt makers, American and Canadian weavers seem to have been familiar with the same patterns, and nothing seems to distinguish patterns with a southern provenance. Whereas quilts and counterpanes were made in part on a quilting frame or large embroidery frame, and a group of women could be involved in the quilting process, a woven coverlet was made on a loom by one person. Home weavers were men as well as women, but one documented overshot coverlet (cat. 16) was made by a woman. A successful woven coverlet, whether overshot or a plain weave (cat. 12 and 13), also required training, dexterity, and an aesthetic sense, especially in the use of colors. There were many professional weavers, making it difficult to distinguish the home products from the professional.

While the dated bedcovers provide a time frame for the use and popularity of pattern designs, they further help to provide a time reference for the types of printed fabrics available to the southern quilt maker. A wide variety of fabrics is found in these quilts and counterpanes, from the plain white cotton grounds, to the complex painted and printed India cottons, used in palampores,[1] to copperplate and woodblock-printed fabrics. Early in the nineteenth century, roller printing began to replace copperplate printing, producing more elaborate designs more quickly. While a few of the cotton prints may be French imports, most are English. Wools, silks, and velvets were also imported.

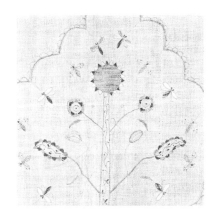

Fig. 3. Detail of embroidery, cat. 6.

Documentary evidence for early bedcoverings

The MESDA research files contain a wealth of information about textiles and all of the components of bedding needed to prepare a bedstead for sleeping such as mattresses, featherbeds, bolsters, pillows and pillowcases, sheets, and blankets. But the documentation of the "bed furniture," the outer visible textiles such as the valance, tester, curtains, headcloth, flounce, and bedcovering, is equally intriguing. A fully dressed bedstead was a valuable possession; it was a status symbol that often provided a very

colorful element in the chamber. It is obvious that the outer bed-covering — the quilt, coverlet, or counterpane — was the most likely piece of the ensemble to survive, probably because of its decorative qualities and its sentimental value for the maker. Although this exhibition concentrates specifically on the surviving decorative outermost bedcoverings, the research data, which is too extensive to discuss here, shows that these other components were also very important elements in a household.

Quilts

One of the earliest mentions of the word *quilt* appears in a 1656 estate appraisal in Northumberland, Virginia, as "1 Quilt."[2] At that time a "quilt" would have been a two- or three-layer whole-cloth bedcovering, constructed of widths of the same plain or printed top fabric seamed together, plus a backing fabric, and perhaps a filler of cotton or wool, that were then quilted together in a decorative pattern (fig. 4). Specific quilt references have been extracted from Maryland, Virginia, North Carolina, South Carolina, and Georgia records. Sometimes fabrics used for quilts are described; they range from calico, "sattin," silk, cotton, and "humkums," to perhaps the most unusual, leather.[3] There are also descriptions of different colors of linings, what we now call the backing.

Quilts that are specifically called "patchwork" are not found in MESDA documents until the sec-

7

ond half of the eighteenth century. The earliest reference recorded by MESDA appears in the estate appraisal of Philip Thomas from Anne Arundel County, Maryland, in 1763: "1 New Patchwork Quilt 3 0 0 / 1 old White Callico D[itt]o. 1 [0 0] / 1 D[itt]o. Patchwork 0 12 0."[4] The "old" patchwork quilt, which has a much lower value than the "New Patchwork Quilt," implies that the former was made many years before the estate

Fig. 4. Detail, eighteenth-century wholecloth quilt, cat. 9.

appraisal was made. Significantly, Philip Thomas's wife, Ann Thomas, was the executrix; she was probably quite capable of clarifying the relative ages and values of these three pieces.

There are few descriptions of patchwork quilt patterns, but an especially early one is found in an 1808 bill of sale of personal property that included "two quilts Made with patchwork one a Sexagon (or so dominated) the other of Squares of Callico and muslin."[5] The second is obviously made of cotton. But little is known about the availability and dissemination of patchwork patterns or quilting patterns.

Apparently patterns for quilting or embroidering counterpanes had some value, because in 1773 a Maryland estate appraisal listed "1 Patern of a Work'd Bed Quilt [£]–.10.–."[6] In 1817 a Mrs. Littleford advertised in a Lexington, Kentucky, newspaper that she "hopes by her attention to the improvement of her young pupils, to merit a continuance of the public patronage. Toilettes and Coverlets drawn for work in the most elegant patterns."[7]

In most estate records, bed-coverings of any kind are rarely described in detail, but theft notices for quilts often provide surprisingly visual descriptions of the stolen articles. Such is the case in a 1799 robbery and reward notice from Hagerstown, Maryland, where the quilt-top fabrics and the quilting patterns are both recorded: "THREE DOLLARS REWARD. STOLEN from the subscriber's tavern, on the Saturday evening before Christmas, two BED QUILTS, one entirely new, chiefly made of dark calicoe and white muslin, with a dark border of furniture calicoe; quilted in single diamonds — the other a light middle, with a dark border, quilted in waves."[8] Another from Savannah, Georgia, of 1818 says: "Robbery. Stolen out of the house of the subscriber, on the 2nd instant, between the hours of 10 and 11 o'clock, a black leather trunk, containing as far as recollected four quilts without borders or linings, a part of a wilson quilt not put together; one of the former in stars, one of cross bar work, one of patch work and the other feathered, with a quantity of other articles."[9] It is noteworthy that the quilts were stored in a trunk during the warm weather. A similar robbery took place in Virginia in 1819: "ROBBERY!! Twenty Dollars Reward. ON the night of the 1st instant, about 7 or 8 o'clock, when the family were at Tea in the adjoining room, some villain came into the passage of the Subscriber's house, went up stairs into a bed-room, and stole a FEATHER BED, Bolster, 2 Pillows, with 1 Linen and 1 Cotton Case,

2 Blankets, and a large Patch Work Bed-Quilt, with the figure of a large Bird perched on the branches of a tree, for a centre piece — The above reward will be paid for the recovery of the Goods and Thief, or for the goods only, Ten Dollars, with all reasonable charges. Robert Chapman."[10] This is a good indication of the bedding in use in a home during a colder month of the year, February. Two early nineteenth-century examples in the exhibition, cat. 21 and 22, have a center medallion format of birds in a "tree," very likely similar to the quilt being described here. In this quilt, the "patch work" was probably appliqué, although in the eighteenth century "patch work" referred to any type of design using patches of cloth, both pieced and appliquéd.

For an appliquéd bedcovering, the designs are cut out of patterned or solid color fabrics and then sewn, or "applied," to the white top either with decorative or blind stitches. In the late eighteenth and early nineteenth centuries, often the images printed on the fabric, such as birds or trees, were individually cut out and then appliquéd in a technique called cut-out chintz appliqué. By the mid-nineteenth century appliqué using solid colors or small overall prints such as those used in the North Carolina Lily pattern (cat. 26, fig. 5), became common. Appliquéd bedcoverings could be quilted or not.

The better known use of the term *patchwork* is for pieced quilts made of various colors and patterns of fabrics cut into shapes and then sewn together,

Fig. 5. Detail, appliqué used on North Carolina Lily quilt, cat. 26.

thereby making a top of many pieces. The earliest known in the United States are from the second half of the eighteenth century, and they continued to be made throughout the nineteenth century (cat. 31). The 1877 *Ladies' Guide to Needle Work, Embroidery, Etc.,* by S. Annie Frost, has a short chapter on patchwork and makes some interesting observations on its history. About this technique the author writes, "It is generally our first work and our last — the schoolgirl's little fingers setting their first crowded or straggling stitches of appalling length in patchwork squares, while the old woman, who can no longer conquer the intricacies of fine work, will still make patchwork quilts for coming generations." After stating that "The taste [for patchwork] is one that has nearly died out," she concludes, "It is a great improvement upon the huge and unwieldy quilting frames of the days of our grandmothers, to make the patchwork for a quilt in bound squares. Each one is lined, first with wadding, then with calico quilted neatly, and bound with strips of calico. These squares being sewn together, the quilt is complete. Album quilts made in this way, with the name of the giver neatly written upon a small square of white in the centre of each piece, are much more acceptable than when they must all be quilted together in a huge frame."[11]

It is unusual to find surviving documented examples of both appliquéd and patchwork quilts, full-size and child-size, all from one family. Four of the quilts in the exhibition are especially well docu-

9

mented by inscribed labels and family history. They were made within the same South Carolina county by Harriet Kirk Marion and her daughter, Catherine Couturier Marion Palmer, for specific people between the years 1830 and 1848.

The women were members of a relatively prominent South Carolina family. Harriet Kirk Marion was the second wife of Francis Dwight Marion (born Francis Dwight, but took the name Marion after his mother's brother, General Francis "Swamp Fox" Marion; he was formally adopted by the general in 1795). They were married in 1801 and lived at Belle Isle Plantation, St. John's Parish, Berkeley County, South Carolina. This is where General Francis Marion is buried. Francis Dwight Marion's first wife was Louisa Kirk, the sister of Harriet (there seems to be no issue from that marriage). Their parents were Gideon Kirk and Rebecca Couturier, widow of Peter Couturier (her maiden name was also Couturier). Catherine Couturier Marion was born 10 April 1807 and married John Gendron Palmer 11 February 1830. Their daughter Harriet Marion Palmer was born 29 November 1830; she married Francis Marion Dwight on 21 August 1850.[12]

The women of this family, over several generations, seem to have been ambitious quilters. In 1830 Harriet Marion pieced and quilted a child-sized quilt for her granddaughter (cat. 17). Ten years later she began the pieced quilt with a honeycomb pattern that was marked and quilted by her great-

Fig. 6. Appliquéd quilt block made by Eliza Catherine Palmer, cat. 20.

granddaughter, Kate Palmer Logare, at a later date (cat. 18). Also represented are an elaborate central medallion quilt (cat. 19), and a friendship quilt of twenty-five blocks put together by friends and relatives in 1847, probably for the marriage of Catherine Couturier Marion Palmer's daughter Harriet Marion Palmer. Each block is signed by the maker (some women made more than one block). A portrait of the Yeadon family (cat. 20a) shows two women who contributed to this quilt, Mary Videau Yeadon (Catherine Palmer's sister) and her adopted daughter, Eliza Catherine Palmer, whose quilt block is shown in figure 6. According to family tradition, Eliza supposedly demonstrated her superior quilting skills by stitching a quilt backwards and left-handed.[13]

Coverlets

The term *coverlet* or *coverlid* is used throughout the eighteenth and nineteenth centuries as a general term for a bedcovering. It is a corruption of the French words *couvre* and *lit*, which refer to something that covers the bed. It was used for coverings that were merely decorative as well as for some that were intended to provide warmth. Some are described as wool or cotton, some as solid colors, some as "patch work," and some as patterned fabrics, as is found in a 1768 Maryland estate inventory which lists "1 Bird Ey'd Coverled."[14] Bird's-eye was any cloth woven in a small pattern that resembled a bird's eye.

Woven coverlets

Bedcoverings that were all wool or wool with linen or cotton were intended for warmth as well as for decoration. Examples presented here range from the very warm bed "rugg" (fig. 7)[15] to the moderately warm overshot coverlets, to the lighter cotton or cotton and wool plaid coverlets. The milder southern climate may help to explain why it seems that so few heavy and warm woven bedcoverings with a southern provenance have been documented.

MESDA has recorded more than 1,600 weavers in the Index of Artisans. A cursory sampling of these records indicates that while most of these professional weavers were men, some were women, and some of the weavers were also dyers. Even though it is often difficult to know what fibers were being woven, many of these weavers had wool on hand as well as linen and cotton.

It is not surprising that instruction books for weavers were available. In 1792 there was an advertisement in a Baltimore newspaper for a book that was to be printed by subscription:

> *A singularly valuable Publication, intended to diffuse manufacturing Knowledge amongst the Weavers of these States (never before made public either in Europe or America) entitled, THE WEAVER'S DRAUGHT-BOOK, AND CLOTHIER's ASSISTANT. . . and Instructions for sleying each Piece and fixing and preparing Cotton Warps. These*

Fig. 7. Detail, woven bed rug, cat. 11.

> *Draughts will include the most useful and esteemed Patterns that are now imported, amongst which will be found a Variety of small and beautiful Diapers, Counterpanes, figured Stuffs, Dimities, Ducapes, Denims, Mock-Marseilles, Cantoons, Corduroys, Velverets, Velvelures, Rib and Jeans, Thicksets, Satinets, Mustinets, several elegant Cords, &c. &c. &c.*[16]

Some of these patterns could easily have been used to produce fabric that could be made into a counterpane or coverlet.

In 1820 an advertisement for another book on "Weaving and Dyeing" was published in the *Raleigh Register*: "AMONGST other books lately received, J. Gales has the Domestic Manufacturer's Assistant, in the arts of Weaving and Dyeing, comprehending a plain system of Directions applying to these arts and other branches nearly connected with them in the manufacture of Cotton and Woolen goods; including many useful Tables and Drafts, in calculating and forming various kinds and patterns of Goods, designed for the improvement of Domestic Manufactures. By J. & R. Bronson."[17]

A common weaving technique of the early nineteenth century was an overshot weave — a fabric with a cotton or linen warp and weft with a supplemental wool pattern weft. The resulting fabric (depending on the weight of the yarns) could be used for carpets or bedcoverings. When assembled in strips and seamed together for a bedcovering it was also called a coverlet; it continues commonly to be called an "overshot coverlet." Most home-woven coverlets were overshot, produced on a four-harness loom, making a great variety of geometric patterns possible. Some early hand-delineated paper drafts have the pattern names written on them, such as "Scattered apples" or "Snow Banks" (fig. 8). Some modern samples were woven from the draft patterns by weaver Ruth Jelks (fig. 9).

Bed Rugs

Rugs or "ruggs" appear in early southern records from the seventeenth century and seem to have lost popularity by the late eighteenth century, although they were still being made in the nineteenth century (see cat. 11). The term is often spelled "rugg" and is usually listed on inventories with other bedding, but the combination "bed rug," as we call them now, was not used. A "Rugg Coverlid" is mentioned in a 1745 Frederick

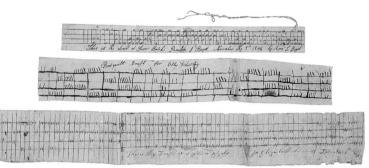

Fig. 8. WEAVING DRAFTS, *American, from a group of twelve in the Old Salem collection, mid-nineteenth century.* INK ON PAPER, COTTON THREAD. *Acc. 1051.*

TOP: "This is the draft of Snow Banks Penelope J. Boyd November the 9th 1846 by Ann L. Boyd." (15 1/4" x 1 5/7"). MIDDLE: "Bed quilt for Draft for Elly Whitley." (18 1/2" x 2 5/8"). The name "Mary An Whitley" appears on some of the other drafts. BOTTOM: "This is the Draft of Scattered apples. Mrs. Elizabeth Stubbs December 1st 1837." (23 1/4" x 3 1/8"). It seems to be written on part of the back of a letter beginning "Plymouth July 21, 1837."

These slips of paper indicated how the loom should be set up to produce specific weaving patterns. Modern samples of "Scattered apples" and "Snow Banks" have been woven from them. While these drafts have no southern history and the women, although named, are anonymous to us, the fact that they are dated is important. It is also significant that although these are clearly patterns for woven bedcoverings, one is still called a "quilt" by the maker.

County, Virginia, estate appraisal, however.[18] One of the earliest mentions is the 1665 estate inventory of Thomas Keelinge, Norfolk County, Virginia: "Two fetherbeds one boulster two pillowes two Blanketts one Greene Rugge greene Curtaines and valians beinge old and the bedstead. . . ."[19] In addition to the green specified here, the rugs in other records were described in various other colors, such as red, blue, and gray. Silk rugs are found in Maryland in 1717/18 and in Virginia in 1723/4 and 1743.[20] Three visually interesting seventeenth-century descriptions, all from Virginia, are: "one Shagg Rugge"; "To a Camell haire Red Rugg" (this rugg was valued at 16 shillings, while a "Round Dutch Table" in the same inventory was valued at 10 shillings); and "2 old Irish Ruggs."[21]

The only use for rugs other than bedding that has been found is an accounting of a Mrs. Durant for the settlement of the estate of one John Culle: "To the Trubell of my House and the Lone of my

12

bedding: and a Ruge he was bured in."[22]

Even though "ruggs" were generally waning in popularity by the last quarter of the eighteenth century, they are among the provisions of the new tavern in Salem, North Carolina, in 1785. The tavern's extensive inventory was divided into categories, and under "Bedding and Linen Things" are "6 green Rugs / 2 Ditto / 1 speckled Rug." According to the Salem Diacony Journal, one of the many documents of the Moravian church that recorded details of daily life in the town, the rugs were purchased in Pennsylvania.[23] While the inventory is written in German script, "Rugs" and "Rug" are in English script. "New" rugs were periodically added to the inventory, but they disappear from the yearly inventories by 1814. An interesting change in the bedding is seen in the "Bedding and Linen" inventory for 1808. Along with "17 double feather beds" and "17 double straw mattresses," "17 woolen coverlets" are listed. These are differentiated from other bedding such as "3 new blankets, 8 poorer, . . . 3 bedquilts . . . 12 counterpanes . . . 4 good rugs, 9 poorer."[24] Bed rugs were apparently still being used, but were consistently replaced by newer and perhaps more "modern" bedding to accommodate the many travelers who stopped at the Salem tavern. The Salem Diacony Journal does not indicate the sources for these new items. By the end of the eighteenth century, "ruggs" and woven coverlets seem to be more

Fig. 9 WEAVING SAMPLES *based on the drafts shown in figure 8.* LEFT: *Scattered Apples draft.* RIGHT: *Snow Banks.*

popular in the backcountry regions than in other areas. For instance, a 1778 Shenandoah County, Virginia, estate inventory accounts for "two woolen Coverleads £6 three Ruggs £6."[25]

Counterpanes

Numerous records refer to "counterpanes," or as it often appears, "counterpins." This term was probably the most frequently used, and apparently meant any variety of bedcoverings. The earliest mention of "counterpane" found to date in MESDA's gleanings comes from a Lancaster County, Virginia, inventory of 1690/91.[26] This is a very rich and descriptive inventory for textiles, especially bedding. Among the items listed are "A Suite of painted Callico Curtains and Counterpane. . . A Sute [*sic*] of Lemon Colour'd damask Curtains, Vallins, head Cloth and Counterpane, with Cradle cloth. . . A Sute [*sic*] of white Callico Curtains & Vallins with fringe & Counterpane. . . ." Here it appears that the bed furniture, including the counterpane, was considered as a "set," and all three are very different. The "painted callico" would have been the popular painted and/or printed cotton from India, the intricate and colorful designs that inspired the development of woodblock printing in England, France and Holland. The "white Callico" was also probably a plain cotton from India. Trade between England and India had been flourishing since 1600 when the East India Company was founded, thus beginning Anglo-

13

Indian commerce and giving England access to these exotic fabrics.

In 1719, another Virginia inventory contained the reference to "one Silk Needle worked Counter pain,"[27] which seems to be a silk-embroidered counterpane. From 1799 comes another reference listing a wide variety of counterpanes, again from Virginia: "One yellow counterpin one chince counter pin one old calico counterpin . . . one white counterpin with fringes one home made counterpin striped."[28] It is interesting that yellow, calico, and white are the same combination listed for the John Carter household in the late seventeenth century.[29]

An estate sale from York County, South Carolina, in 1822 gives a good comparative listing of quilts and counterpanes for the early nineteenth century. Some quilts are grouped together and then valued, "3 Quilts $14.00. . . Bed Quilts $2.00." Others are "1 Bed Quilt Patched Quilt 4.00, 1 D[itt]o D[itt]o 5.00," and "Quilt .75." There were two "checked" counterpanes, each valued at $1.65. But the four others ranged in value from $10.00 for "1 [Counterpane] flowered with needle," to $12.62 1/2 for "1 Counterpane."[30]

All-white bedcoverings have a white cotton or linen top, and the decorative elements are often achieved by stuffing and cording, sometimes combined with a quilted background. White-worked counterpanes can be embellished with white embroi-

Fig. 10. Scissors.

Top: *probably English, late eighteenth or early nineteenth century. Stamped "J.E.B." Steel; 4 3/4" x 1 3/4". Acc. 4143.*
Bottom: *probably English, late eighteenth or early nineteenth century. Steel; 2 3/4" x 1 5/8". Acc. 317.2.*

dery stitches, either simple or elaborate, or with candle-wicking.[31] In many of the early records describing bedcoverings, "white" is often followed by "counterpane" or "counterpin." In many areas of the country, fine decorative stitching on a white ground continued to be a popular treatment for lightweight bedcoverings into the nineteenth century. But it is interesting to note that of all the bedcoverings recorded and documents examined by MESDA, the predominance of references to white bedcoverings and to the term *counterpane* is from Virginia.

White-worked counterpanes, in a descending order of value, are also described in 1811 in Ludenburg, Virginia, as "1 White worked Counterpin 2.–.; 1 W. Counterpin 1. 4.–; 1 ditto 1. 4.–; 1 ditto 1. 16.–." This list goes on to describe " 1 Patch Work & Counterpin 1. 16. –. And 1 Home spun ditto 1. 4.–."[32] Again, "counterpane," meaning a bedcovering, takes on a different meaning depending on the description. Here the one with the highest value seems to be embroidered, the next three are perhaps plain white; a patchwork design is valued equal to one of the plain counterpanes, and then the final one, a simple "homespun" fabric, has the same value as each of the plain white ones.

Counterpanes seem to be either linen or, more likely, cotton. Cotton and linen counterpanes are listed in the will of Mildred Stewart of Virginia in

Fig. 11. QUILTING FRAME, *yellow pine, mid-nineteenth century with later alterations;* 102" l. x 40 1/2" w. x 36 5/8" h. *Acc. 2673.*

This type of quilting frame conserved space in a household because most of the quilt could be rolled up on the rollers, exposing only the narrow width of the top that was being worked for quilting. The rather roughly shaped ends of the frame are original and have a very architectural quality. The bases and rollers are replacements. The original gear and ratchet arrangement at the end of each roller was probably wood.

1813 where, among other household items she leaves to her brother William "a yarn and cotton counterpin," to her brother Westly "a new Huckaback Counterpin," and to her friend Benjamin Grymes "a Bed quilt."[33] The "huckaback" would have been a woven patterned linen that was also often used for toweling or table linens. Here the two "counterpins" are apparently not quilted, but lighter-weight bedcoverings as compared with the "Bed quilt."

There is also evidence that fabrics produced specifically for bedcoverings, as well as finished quilts and decorative counterpanes, were being imported, especially in Charleston, South Carolina. In 1750 a newspaper notice in Charleston lists an assortment of goods just imported from London and being sold by Benjamin Dart: "A variety of woollen and other goods suitable to the season, also printed and white callicoes and linnens, India painted and plain chints, ginghams and Irish linnens, large figur'd cottons for beds, with silk and thread bindings, which, with many other useful articles, are to be sold very cheap, at their store in Traad-

street."[34] About the same time, in 1753, Benjamin Stead was also advertising finished goods in Charleston: "JUST IMPORTED in the Nancy, Capt. Brown from London, and to be sold cheap. . . matrasses and bed quilts."[35] These would have been whole-cloth quilts. No doubt costly, bedcoverings made of India silk were also being imported to Charleston via London: "TWO very NEAT, RICH, and CURIOUS INDIA SILK COUNTERPANES, / To be DISPOSED of by / WEBB & DOUGHTY. / Who have just imported per the America, Captain Rainer, / from London."[36]

The effect of fine quilting was still in demand in the late eighteenth and early nineteenth centuries and gave rise to the popularity of an imported loom-woven white fabric that imitated skilled hand-quilting, called Marseilles (after the city in France where it was developed) or Marcelle. William and George Hall advertised in Charleston in 1806 that they had for sale at the store "An elegant assortment of MARSEILLES, KNOTTED AND PRINTED COUNTERPANES."[37]

Quilt makers

Only five professional quilters have been recorded in the MESDA Index of Artisans. All five are women who were paid to quilt designs on whole cloth. The person contracting for their services would supply the materials, and the quilter would assemble and quilt it.[38] It is also possible that an already assembled quilt was brought to the quilter, who quilted it for a fee. They were all working in the 1730s and 1740s. Three of them were from Annapolis, Maryland, one from Charleston, South Carolina, and one from Westmoreland, Virginia. It is clear from the advertisements that they were quilting clothing as well as bedcoverings. For instance, a Charleston, South Carolina, newspaper advertisement from 1735 announces, "Mrs. Grenier living at Mr. Samuel Glaser's in Broad-street gives Notice that she perform's all sorts of quilted Work, Petticoats, Coverlets &c. in a nice manner; she also makes Umbrelloes of all sorts of stuff, at a reasonable rate."[39]

At least one quilter had enough work to employ a helper. Sarah Monro, who was probably English, advertised herself in Annapolis in 1745 as offering "Quilting of all Kinds, whether fine or coarse, such

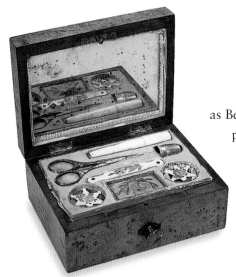

Fig. 12. SEWING BOX, *American or English, c. 1820. Burlwood, ivory, mother of pearl, paper, velvet, and glass mirror; 2 3/8" x 5 1/4" x 3 7/8" Acc. 421.2.*

This burlwood sewing box belonged to Christina Vogler of Salem, North Carolina (fig. 13). The initials "CV" are engraved in a piece of mother of pearl inlaid in the top. Christina was the mother of Lisetta Vogler Fries, who made a Washington Sidewalk quilt (cat. 35). She apparently gave this sewing box to Lisetta, because on a small piece of paper in the bottom of the box is written: "This Box & Contents belongs to L. M. Fries." On another paper is written the order of service for "Father's funeral" on 2 August 1863. Inside the ivory needle box, along with various size sewing needles, is a silver bodkin engraved with the initials "LVM".

as Bed-Quilts, Gowns, Petticoats &c. performed in the best and neatest Manner, by the Subscriber, at her House in Annapolis, as well as in England, and much cheaper."[40] About eight months later Sarah Monro advertised that her hired quilter had run away, "an English Convict Servant Woman named Elizabeth Crowder, by Trade a Quilter; she is upwards of 40 Years of Age, pretty tall, and round sholder'd, her Hair is very grey, and has been lately cut off; but it is supposed she has got a Tower, to wear instead of it. She had on when she went away a dark striped Cotton and Silk Gown, a blue quilted Coat, blue Worsted Stockings, and black Shoes newly soled: She had with her a large bundle. . . particularly a sprigg'd Linned Gown, Shifts, Caps, Aprons, and other Things unknown."[41]

Elizabeth Crowder may have come from the tradition of quilters as described in the 1747 book, *The London Tradesman. Being a Compendious View of All the Trades, Professions, Arts, both Liberal and Mechanic, now practiced in the Cities of London and Westminster,* by R. Campbell. This book describes nearly 250 trades; two that are mutually supportive are those of the quilter and

16

the pattern-drawer. The craft of the quilter is described in the following way.

Work, and requires Girls of Strength. A Mistress must have a pretty kind of Genius to make them fit well and adjust them to the reigning Mode; but in the main, it is not necessary she should be a Witch.

Since I am so bold as to make free with the Ladies Hoop-Petticoat, I must just peep under the Quiltted-Petticoat. Every one knows the Materials they are made of: They are made mostly by Women, and some Men, who are employed by the Shops and earn but little. They quilt likewise Quilts for Beds for the Upholder. This they make more of than of the Petticoats, but not very considerable, nothing to get rich by, unless they are able to purchase the Materials and sell them finished to the Shops, which few of them do. They rarely take Apprentices, and the Women they employ to help them, earn Three or Four Shillings a Week and their Diet. . . .

While the pattern-drawer certainly did not supply every quilter or embroiderer with patterns, this trade was a creative and helpful one for those who needed it.

Fig. 13. DAGUERREOTYPE, 1851, of John (1783–1881) and Christina (1792–1863) Vogler. *Acc. 86.1.*

Pattern-Drawers are employed in drawing Patterns for the Callico-Printers, for Embroiderers, Lace-workers, Quilters, and several little Branches belonging to Women's Apparel. They draw Patterns upon Paper, which they sell to Workmen that want them. . . . It requires no great Taste in Painting, nor the Principles of Drawing; but a wild kind of Imagination, to adorn their Works with a sort of regular Confusion, fit to attract the Eye but not to please the Judgment. . . .[42]

Other than the above-cited comment that quilting was "nothing to get rich by," there is little evidence for the cost of making bedcoverings, except for a notice in an 1812 Annapolis, Maryland, newspaper:

WOOL COVERS.
This article of domestic manufacture has been introduced into most of our families, in consequence of the scarcity of blankets, produced by the nonintercourse with Britain. As a cheap and comfortable substitute, it merits general attention. The materials can be had without difficulty. It can be made in every family, with one day's work of a seamstress,

17

and will not cost more than $2.75. It is as warm as two blankets, which would cost $2.50 — it is remarkably light and pleasant, and the wool, with a small addition of new wool, may be applied to making a new cover, when the calico of the old one shall be worn out. I have had four made in my house, and find the cost of each not to exceed the above estimate, viz.:

2 pieces of India calico at 6s 6d 5 yds, each	$1 74
3 1/4 lbs. Wool, reducing by carding to 3 lbs. at 40	1 30
Carding 12 1/2 a lb.	37
Quilting in squares of 6 inches, 1 day's work	27
Cotton thread,	6
$3.75.	

A FARMER.[43]

Not only is this significant for the costs associated with the production of the "wool cover," but also for the materials used, the labor involved, the quilting pattern, and the fact that one bed quilt with a wool filler and cotton top was considered equal to two blankets in warmth.

Fig. 14. THIMBLES.

LEFT: *att. John Vogler, Salem, North Carolina, c. 1830. Silver; 3/4" x 1/2" dia. Acc. 3771.* This silver thimble is engraved with the initials "L.V.M." for Lisetta Maria Vogler, daughter of the silversmith John Vogler, who made the pieced quilt illustrated as cat. 35.
RIGHT: *American or English, c. 1830. Brass; 5/8" x 1/2" dia. Acc. T-107.* Inscribed on this thimble is the admonition, "Fear God." It has a Salem, North Carolina, history of ownership.

Tools and Implements

Two large pieces of equipment were needed to produce most of the bed-coverings in this exhibition: a loom for the plaid and over-shot coverlets, and a quilting frame for the quilts. Looms appear in estate records more frequently than quilting frames, which are listed throughout the eighteenth century. For instance, among the items in the estate of William Blaikley from Williamsburg, Virginia, are "one Large Quilting fraim one small Ditto. . . two Counterpains not finished."[44] A quilting frame could be as simple as four long narrow boards that formed a rectangle that were supported on the backs of chairs, to a more decorative type, such as the example in the exhibition (fig. 11), which has two shaped base ends and two long rollers attached to them.

The other tools quilters or embroiderers used are seldom mentioned in the documentary records. This is probably because these needleworking implements were given by mother to daughter, or to other family members or close friends. This was the case in the Moravian community of Salem, North Carolina. The implements in this exhibition are all from the Old Salem collection, and many have a family history.

One of the most beautiful sewing-related items in the exhibit is a small work-box (fig. 12) from around 1820, that belonged to Christina Vogler, whose picture appears in figure 13, and later to her daughter Lisetta Vogler Fries, who made the quilt shown as cat. 35. It contains an ivory needlebox (complete with Lisetta's initialed bodkin), ivory painted thread holders, scissors, and a thimble. Two other tiny thimbles (fig. 14), one engraved with Lisetta Vogler's initials and one with the admonition "Fear God" in relief, are proof of the young age at which girls began to perfect their sewing skills.

Other implements that made the seamstress' life easier include sewing clamps (fig. 15) and thread boxes (fig. 16). Local cabinetmakers turned sewing clamps, which were then available to be purchased. Usually the padded pincushion was attached to the base, but some, like the one illustrated, also provided storage for thread and other small accoutrements in a box with a pincushion top. The sewing clamp could be easily attached to the edge of a table or the arm of a chair to hold needles and pins close at hand. Many round indentations on the underside of the edge of a table are a tell-tale sign that the table was often used to attach a sewing clamp.

Fig. 15. SEWING CLAMP, *attributed to the cabinetmaker Karsten Petersen (1776–1858), Salem, North Carolina. Cherry, walnut, cardboard, silk, and gilded paper, 1820–1840. 2 1/4" x 6 3/4". Acc. 2089.4.*

The padded black silk pincushion and the sides of the box, covered with black paper, are decorated with small bouquets of flowers and, on one side of the box, an oval floral wreath. The decoration is nearly identical to that on another sewing clamp in Old Salem's collection said to have been painted by the Salem artist Daniel Welfare (1796–1841).

The tall turned thread box shown in figure 16 is functional as well as decorative. It separates into several compartments: one at the bottom to hold thread, which would have been dispensed through the ivory bosses, one in the middle for needles, and one at the top for a thimble.

A variety of needle cases were used by the women and girls of Salem (fig. 17). The earliest example shown here, from 1838, is embroidered silk; it serves as a pincushion as well as a needle case. The embroidery is typical of the high quality of fancy needlework that was taught in the Salem Girls Boarding School. In the mid-nineteenth century, sewing implements of vegetable ivory also became popular; a needle case of this material is shown here. Another pincushion-needle case, from the late nineteenth century, was made in Salem. It has a watercolor-painted cover showing the Moravian Church in Salem, which must have been a popular subject, because there are several similar ones known.

All of the implements included here have a Salem history of use, ownership, or manufacture; occasionally these necessary items appear in records from other areas. Not only did Barbara Ocker of Frederick County, Maryland have "1 Set flying Shettle & Lathe 1.00, 2 Shettles .12 1/2, 1 Swift .40,. . . 2 Setts Gears & 1 Reed 1.00. . ." (suggesting activity as a weaver), but she also had "1 Chest &

Needle Book 1.50, 1 Tin Cups Containing Patches & 2 Broken silver Rings .10, 1 Japanned Box & needle case .06 1/2, 1 Lot of Patches & thread .25, 1 Small Box & thread .12 1/2, 1 Lot of Patches & 1 Pr. Small Scissars .18 3/4. . ."[45] She very well could have been a professional needle-worker and weaver.

The recording of sewing implements in official records is rare. More frquently, smaller utilitarian items appear in personal records such as letters, diaries, and individual household records. An excellent example is the "Notes Memorandum Receipts" kept by Julia Clark, the wife of William Clark of Lewis and Clark fame, in 1820. Her small memo-randum book records personal possessions (such as clothing and jewelry) that she took with her when she, her children, and her husband returned to Virginia from Missouri, where they had been living. Among the items of note were two silver thimbles, a work basket, and a pincushion.[46]

These references can be compared to the guide-lines published in *The Workwoman's Guide,* printed in London in 1838. In one chapter entitled the Work-Box, a "work-box or basket" is described as being large enough "to hold a moderate supply of work," and of an easily portable size. It is further described as having "divisions or partitions, as they assist in keeping it in order." In addition to containing cotton and silk for sewing, tapes, a bobbin, buttons, and hooks and eyes, other essential tools were listed: scissors, a pin cushion, an emery cush-ion, a stiletto (a sharp pointed instrument for making eyelet holes), a bodkin (an instrument with a knob on one end and a large eye on the other for running drawstrings and cording), a thimble, and a small knife. No less than six different types of scissors are described, which would have been helpful for quiltmaking, embroidery and plain sewing: a "large pair, for cutting out linen; a medium size for common use; a smaller pair with sharper points, for cutting out muslin work &c."[47] The two pairs of scissors in figure 10 could correspond with the medium and smaller sizes. *The Work-woman's Guide* also is clear about pincushions. They could be "circular, square, diamond, oblong, or any other shape. Cut out the forms in two cards, both of which are covered with silk. Flannel is put between, and the two sides neatly sewed togeth-er."[48] The two pocket examples in figure 17 are a combination of pincushion and needle case. For stor-ing needles, pieces of kerseymere, a soft twill wool with a nap, were recommended to keep them sorted by size.

These tools, along with the surviving bedcovers, are symbolic of the needleworkers and weavers who created objects that could help keep people comfortable. From the written documents,

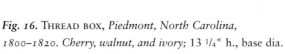

Fig. 16. THREAD BOX, *Piedmont, North Carolina, 1800–1820. Cherry, walnut, and ivory;* 13 1/4" h., base dia. 3 3/8". *Acc. 299.1*

The neoclassical shape of this thread box was popular in the first quarter of the nineteenth century.

20

Fig. 17. Needle cases.

as brief and sometimes curious and conflicting as they are, we get a glimpse of the furnishings of a household, specifically, in this brief study, the bedstead with its covering. Although we will never know exactly what the accommodations were like, or exactly how they changed over time, we can develop a sense of them, from the meager to the grand.

If all the information relating to bedcoverings and bedding in the MESDA research files could be plotted on a map of the South, it would probably reveal significant findings about the material culture of the different regions; a look at appraisal values for bedding could offer even more insight. But the most satisfying aspect of trying to understand these quilts, coverlets, and counterpanes is to be able to see the surviving pieces themselves. While most quiltmakers and home weavers remain anonymous, we are fortunate to know the names and usually some family history for half of the bedcovers presented here, because they are identified either through the maker's own stitched initials or name, a written

Top, left: Embroidered white silk needle case *made by "Lavinia," Salem, North Carolina. 1838. Silk, silver sequins, cardboard, glass mirror; 3 5/8" x 6 5/8". Acc. 4240.11.* On the flaps are embroidered the words, "firm and true" (lower) "such as I feel for you" (upper).
Top, right: Pincushion and needle case, *Salem, North Carolina, c. 1890. Paper, silk, cotton, watercolor; 3 3/8" x 2 3/4" x 7/8". Acc. 3946.* Cotton stuffing covered with pink satin makes the pincushion, and there are two wool "pages" for needles. It ties with pink silk ribbons. The inscription on the back reads "MORAVIAN CHURCH / SALEM, N.C. 1800" (the date the church was built).
Bottom: Needle case, *probably English, c. 1850. Vegetable ivory; 2 1/2" x 3/4". Acc. C-185.* This needle case is threaded in the middle to screw together. Vegetable ivory was a term for tagua, the fruit of the ivory-nut palm (*Phytelephas macrocarpa*), which grows in tropical Central and South America. In the mid-nineteenth century it became popular as a substitute for elephant ivory.

label on the piece itself, or through family history. We also have portraits of six of them, making their work even more personal and timeless.

These quilts and counterpanes were made by women, or groups of women, in a home environment. Those who designed, assembled, embroidered, or quilted these pieces did so because of a family need, whether for warmth or beauty. But the final result is a testament to a keen eye, a creative flair, an experienced needle, and an investment of time. We know that each woman made at least one quilt in her lifetime, and more than likely several, as is the case with some of the makers in this exhibition. It is our good fortune that we can meet these women through an expressive but useful piece that has created for each of them a legacy — the humble bedcovering — that now, through this exhibition, has become art.

21

Notes

1. The word *palampore* comes from the Persian and Hindi, *palangposh,* meaning a bedcover. Florence M. Montgomery, *Textiles in America 1650-1870.* (New York, W. W. Norton & Company, 1984), 314.

2. Estate of Ralph Horsley, *Northumberland County, Virginia, Record Book 1652-1658,* 1 Sept. 1656, p. 90a.

3. "Calico" as defined by Florence Montgomery in *Textiles in America 1650-1870* is "cotton cloth of many grades and varieties first made in India and later in the West" (p. 184). "Humkum" is probably "humhum," defined by Montgomery as "plain cotton of thick, stout texture woven in Bengal" (p. 262). For a reference to leather quilts, see the the inventory of John Carter cited in note 26.

4. Estate of Philip Thomas, *Maryland Prerogative Court, vol. 84, Inventories, 1764,* p. 79, 13 March 1763.

5. *Frederick County, Virginia, Deed Book 31, 1808-09,* 29 Sept. 1808, pp. 232-33.

6. Estate of Nicholas Riley of Kent County, *Maryland Prerogative Court, vol. III, Inventories, 1773,* 5 March 1773, p. 321.

7. *Kentucky Gazette,* Lexington, Kentucky, 22 Nov. 1817.

8. *The Maryland Herald & Elizabeth Town Advertiser,* Hager's Town, Maryland, 17 January 1799. "Furniture calicoe" is a cotton print intended for upholstery or curtains, which would probably have had a larger print design than calico intended for clothing.

9. *The Savannah Republican,* Georgia, 3 Sept. 1818. It is not known what is meant by a "wilson quilt."

10. *American Beacon and Norfolk & Portsmouth Daily Advertiser,* Virginia, 3 February 1819.

11. S. Annie Frost, *The Ladies' Guide to Needle Work, Embroidery, Etc.: Being a Complete Guide to All Kinds of Ladies' Fancy Work* (New York, 1877; reprint, Mendocino, Calif.: R.L. Shep, 1986), 128.

12. Information on the makers of these quilts was collected from census and court records by Carol Williams Gebel for MESDA in 1991.

13. Personal communication, Videau K. F. Simons, great-great-granddaughter of Eliza Catherine Palmer.

14. Estate of Hezekiah Anderson of Worcester County, *Maryland Prerogative Court, vol. 98, Inventories, 1768-1769,* 18 March 1768, p. 332.

15. "Indeed the word rug is believed to have come from the Scandinavian word *ryijys,* meaning a rough material, a frieze." From *Bed Ruggs / 1722-1833* (Hartford, Conn.: Wadsworth Atheneum, 1972), 11. *The Oxford English Dictionary* (vol. R, 876) also gives Scandinavian origins for *rug,* specifically from a Norwegian dialect, as *rugga* or *rogga,* meaning coarse coverlet.

16. *The Maryland Journal and Baltimore Advertiser,* 16 March 1792. John Hargrove, *The Weavers Draft Book and Clothiers Assistant* (Baltimore, 1792), reprinted in facsimile with an introduction by Rita J. Drosko (Worcester, Mass.: American Antiquarian Society, 1979).

17. *Raleigh Register,* North Carolina, 21 April 1820.

18. Estate of Elinor Phipp, 25 June 1745, *Frederick Co., Virginia, Will Book no. 1 [with Inventories & Accounts], 1743-1751.* Together with two other items of bedding, "one Blankit. . . Bedtick," the rugg was valued at 15 shillings.

19. Estate of Thomas Keelinge, *Norfolk County, Virginia, Wills & Deeds, Book E, 1666-75,* 29 Aug. 1665, p. 6a.

20. Estate of Thomas Reed, planter of Talbot County, *Maryland Prerogative Court, vol. 1, Inventories, 1718,* 13 Feb. 1717/18. p. 1; estate of John Smith, *Deeds, Wills and Orders, Elizabeth City County, Virginia, 1723-1730,* 19 Feb. 1723/24, p. 2; and estate of Richard Kirkland, *Will Book A, Pt. 1, 1742-52, Fairfax County, Virginia,* 18 Oct. 1743, p. 31.

21. Estate of Andrew Bodnam, *Norfolk County, Virginia, Wills & Deeds, Book E, 1666-75,* 17 Oct. [no year; among the entries for 1666], p. 7a; estate of Thomas Teackle, *Accomack County, Virginia, Wills &c. 1692-1715,* 18 Aug. 1696, p. 138a; estate of John Davis, Henrico County, *Virginia, Record Book No. 5, (Deeds, Wills, &c.) 1688-97,* 15 Nov. 1689 (transcript), p. 101.

22. This account was submitted in May Court, 1690, and is contained in *North Carolina Higher-Court Records 1670-1696,* pp. 15-16.

23. Tavern Inventory, Salem, North Carolina, 30 April 1784 (translation by Edmund Schwarze); Salem Diacony Journal, 31 Jan. 1785, 30 April 1785. Archives of the Moravian Church of America, Southern Province, Winston-Salem, North Carolina.

24. Salem Tavern Inventory, April 1808.

25. Estate of William Millar, *Shenandoah Co., Virginia, Will Book A, 1772–1784*, 9 Nov. 1778, p. 238.

26. "An Inventory of the. . . Estate of Coll. John Carter (decd)," *Lancaster County, Virginia, Inventories & Wills, No. 8 , 1690–1709*, Jan. 1690/91, p. 21a, 27. Also in this inventory are listed "a leather Quilt" and " An old Leather Quilt."

27. Estate of Anthony Holladay, deceased, *Isle of Wight County, Virginia, Wills, Inventories, &c. 1718–29*, 28 Sept. 1719, p. 8.

28. "Attachment against Nathaniel Smith, at suit of Thomas Kelley. . . ." *Berkeley County, Virginia, Order Book 1799*, 29 Aug. 1799, p. 275.

29. See note 26 for the John Carter household inventory.

30. Estate of Polly Cunningham, 30 March 1822, York Co., *South Carolina, Inventories, Appraisements, and Sales, Book I, 1813–1826*, p. 71.

31. *The Needleworker's Dictionary* defines candlewick, or tufting, as a "form of embroidery worked on a strong linen or cotton, preferably unshrunk, using a thick, soft thread which is named candlewick, as originally it consisted of several cotton wicks plied together. The pattern is outlined in running stitches leaving a loop of thread between each stitch which is then cut. When washed, the fabric shrinks a little and holds the thread tightly."

32. Estate of Armstead W. Jeter, *Ludenburg County, Virginia, Will Book No. 7, 1810–18*, 20 March 1811, p. 27.

33. Estate of Mildred Stewart, *King George County, Virginia, Will Book 3, 1804–46*, 4 June 1813.

34. *South Carolina Gazette*, Charleston, 17 Dec. 1750.

35. *South Carolina Gazette*, Charleston, 24 Sept. 1753.

36. *South-Carolina Gazette*, Charleston, 13 Sept. 1768.

37. *Charleston Courier*, South Carolina, 10 Dec. 1806.

38. The audit of Major Turbevile's estate, 3 Nov. 1744 contained the item: "To pd. Lettice McKenney for quilting and making a Coat for Letty Turbervile p. Rect. Book 0: 7: 9." *Westmoreland County, Virginia, Records & Inventories No. 1, 1723–46*, p. 312.

39. *South Carolina Gazette*, Charleston, 31 May 1735.

40. *The Maryland Gazette*, Annapolis, 26 July 1745.

41. *Ibid.*, Annapolis, 1 April 1746.

42. R. Campbell, *The London Tradesman: Being a Compendious View of All the Trades, Professions, Arts, both Liberal and Mechanic, now practiced in the Cities of London and Westminster* (London, 1747), 115 and 213.

43. *The Maryland Republican*, Annapolis, 29 Jan. 1812.

44. Estate of William Blaikley, *York County, Virginia, Wills and Inventories, No. 18, part 1, 1732–1740*, 21 June 1736, p. 297.

45. Estate of Barbara Ocker, 11 October 1820, *Frederick County, Maryland, Register of Wills (Inventories) 1819–1821*, HS 4, i, p. 348.

46. *Clark's Other Journal*, ed. Robert G. Stone and David M. Hinkley (Lee's Summit, Mo.: Fat Little Pudding Boys Press, 1995), 11. It is interesting that she also notes the clothes and possessions that she left in Missouri. Among these are "Mrs. Belt has a white counterpin to quilt for me also a cradle quilt to piece" (p. 105).

47. *The Workwoman's Guide, Containing Instructions to the Inexperienced in Cutting Out and Completing Those Articles of Wearing Apparel, &c,. Which Are Usually Made at Home; Also, Explanations on Upholstery, Straw-Platting, Bonnet Making, Knitting, &c*, By a Lady (London: Simpkin, Marshall, and Co., 1838), 15.

48. *Workwoman's Guide*, 213.

Quilts
Coverlets
&
Counterpanes

1. TUFTED CANDLEWICK COUNTERPANE, *made by Priscilla Armistead, near Edenton, North Carolina, 1793.* Cotton candlewicking on a cotton twill ground; 83" x 74", plus 6 ¹/₂" fringe. *Acc. 3173.*

The initials of the maker and the date, "AUGUST THE 16 + 1793 PA," *prominently surround the center oval medallion of this counterpane. It is one of the earliest known surviving southern bedcovers with candlewicking. Each of its four sides has a complex but symmetrical design of a basket of stylized flowers, with twining vines* that extend to the stylized fleur-de-lis that accents each corner. Swags with tassels surround the center motif. This cotton counterpane has its original ball-and-tassel fringe on three sides.

—————————

All dimensions are given as height x width.

2. EMBROIDERED AND OPENWORK COUNTERPANE, *made by Amelia Chenoweth Nash, Jefferson County, Kentucky, c. 1800.*
Cotton satin stitch and a variety of openwork patterns on a plain-weave cotton ground, with cotton fringe; 116" x 104". *Acc. 2033.3.*

28

Amelia Chenoweth was the daughter of Captain Richard Chenoweth and his wife Margaret (Peggy) McCarty. She married Col. Harmon Nash on 1 June 1792, the day that Kentucky became a state, making them the first couple married in the new state. This counterpane is a testament to Amelia's superb needleworking skill. It exhibits freedom of design and balance without a rigid adherence to symmetry. A large openwork six-petaled flower, the counter-

pane's central focus, is connected by four undulating leafy stems to the rest of the design. The original fringe on all four sides is intact.

REF: John Bivins and Forsyth Alexander, *The Regional Arts of the Early South* (Winston-Salem, N.C.: MESDA, 1991), 167.

3. EMBROIDERED COUNTERPANE, *descended in the Morris family of Franklin, Tennessee, c. 1800–1810.*
Cotton embroidery on a plain-weave cotton ground; 98 ¹/₂" x 83". *Acc. 3696.*

The central motif of this counterpane is a basket with
a tall vining plant bearing stylized flowers, surrounded
by other plants. A deeply undulating vine serves as the
border. The top and bottom edges are hemmed, but the
other two sides are selvage.

4. TUFTED CANDLEWICK QUILT, *attributed to Virginia, c. 1820.*
Cotton with back, batting, and candlewicking of cotton; 98" x 90". *Acc. 2759.*

30

A stylized three-petaled flower with scrolling leaves, enclosed in a diamond, is the central focus of this quilt. Variations of this flower motif are repeated throughout the symmetrical design. A geometric sawtooth pattern forms the border; the corners at the foot of the coverlet are cut away to accommodate bedposts. The dramatic candlewicking is very dense and deep, and the ground is parallel-quilted in diagonal lines.

5. Stuffed and corded quilt, *attributed to eastern Tennessee, c. 1830.*
Closely woven cotton top with a looser-weave cotton back; 103" x 95". *Acc. 2676.*

A symmetrical and deeply undulating corded vine, connecting stuffed-work grapes and grape leaves, forms the three-dimensional design for this quilt. The grapes *and leaves were stuffed through small holes in the backing material. The background is parallel-quilted all over in diagonal lines.*

6. EMBROIDERED COUNTERPANE, *made by Elizabeth "Bess" Abrams (1782–1863),*
Newberry County, South Carolina, 1807.
Cotton embroidery on a plain-weave cotton ground; cotton fringe;
89 ⁵/₈" x 74 ¹/₄", plus 3 ¹/₂" fringe on the two long sides. *Acc. 1110.2.*

32

This embroidered counterpane is initialed and dated at the head "BA 3 / 1807." The "3" probably indicates the linen number in the household inventory. Bess Abrams was the daughter of James and Mary Abrams; she married William Renwick in 1810. Here the stylized flowers, swags, insects, and vines are embroidered in rose-red, blue, and white cotton, now faded. A delicate fringe decorates the two long sides. For a later pieced quilt by Elizabeth Abrams Renwick, see cat. 33.

7. EMBROIDERED COUNTERPANE, *made by Jane Cooper, Florence, South Carolina, 1823.*
Cotton embroidery on a plain-weave cotton ground; cotton fringe; 93 $\frac{1}{4}$" x 90 $\frac{3}{4}$", plus 1 $\frac{3}{4}$" fringe.
Acc. 3017.

Above the vining circle enclosing the floral central motif of this counterpane, the signature and date are embroidered: "Jane Cooper. November. 28. 1823." The balanced, *restrained design is worked in satin stitch and running stitch in two shades of blue and rose-red cotton thread. Some original fringe remains on three sides.*

8. PAINTED AND DYED COTTON PALAMPORE (DETAIL), *India, 1750–1800.*
Mordant-painted and resist-dyed cotton; 80" x 82 ½". *Acc. 2421.*

This bedcover is made of two pieces sewn together in the center, although a palampore was usually one single chintz panel. The word palampore *comes from the Persian and Hindi,* palangposh, *meaning a bedcover. This example is the result of repeated wax-resist dye baths, mordant painting, and washing typical of India cottons imported by the East India Company since the late seventeenth century. The overall pattern is a trailing vine with a variety of* flowers, leaves, and birds. There is a black fleur-de-lis stamp in one corner. When MESDA acquired this piece, it was quilted to a modern backing (now removed); it therefore still shows signs of the quilting.

REF: This palampore is shown in a period room setting in Bivins and Alexander, *The Regional Arts of the Early South,* 70.

Quilts, Coverlets & Counterpanes

9. WHOLE-CLOTH QUILT, *American, c. 1750–1800.*
Wool with wool batting, back, and quilting thread; 78 ½" x 76". *Acc. 476.1.*

This red wool quilt truly demonstrates the adeptness of the needleworker. Its intricate quilting creates a variety of well-balanced patterns. A circular medallion in a diamond, in a square with rounded corners, makes up the center medallion. Overlapping scallops form a wide border. The diamond-in-a-square motif is also used in the late eighteenth and early nineteenth centuries in pieced and appliquéd quilts.

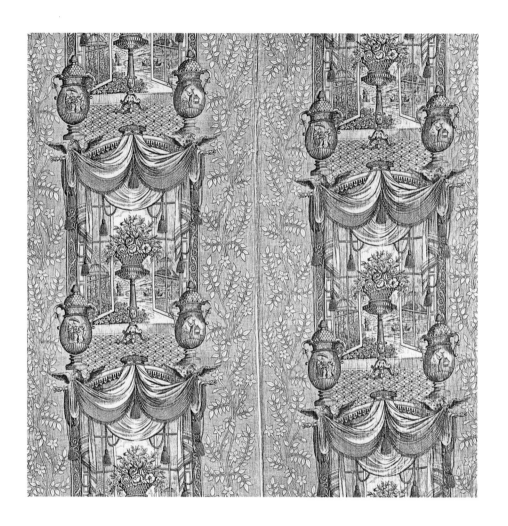

36

This blue roller-printed whole-cloth quilt came from the Daniel Parker family of Charleston and Marlboro County, South Carolina. It is made of four strips of the printed fabric, each about 22 inches wide. It is quilted all over in a diamond pattern. There is no edge binding. The roller-print pattern repeat is 19 inches and shows an open French window framing a basket of flowers on a plant stand, flanked by large chinoiserie-decorated urns. The top of the window is heavily draped and has eagle finials. An all-over pattern of trailing leaves and flowers provides the background on either side of the window.

The technique of engraving patterns on copper cylinders helped to reduce the cost of printing fabrics while allowing much faster production compared to woodblock or copperplate printing. Most furnishing fabrics were produced by this method by 1815. The date of this fabric is confirmed by the close similarity of the draperies, pedestals, and vases to those illustrated in Rudolph Ackermann's 1819 and 1820 Repository of Arts, Literature, Commerce, Manufacture, Fashions and Politics, *a monthly magazine published in London.*

11. WOVEN BED RUG, *attributed to the vicinity of Wytheville, Virginia, 1825.*
Wool and linen; 89 ³/₄" x 73 ³/₄". *Acc. 2175.3.*

This bed rug is initialed and dated "EG" in one corner and "825" in another corner; the '1' from the date 1825 has probably been cut off, as this panel is slightly shorter than the other. This rug is two panels wide, seamed in the center. Its geometric pattern consists of diamonds inside octagons, with diamonds in between, surrounded by a zigzag border. The warp and weft yarns are a two-ply con-struction of a single linen yarn plied with a single woolen yarn; the pattern is achieved by a two-ply wool yarn tied in turkey knots.

REF: This rug is shown in a period room setting in Bivins and Alexander, *Regional Arts of the Early South*, p. 115.

12. WOVEN COVERLET (DETAIL), *Randolph County, North Carolina, 1825–1860.*
Cotton and wool; 92" x 82". *Acc. 3121.1.*

Catalogue nos. 12 and 13 are from a group of similar woven coverlets that have a provenance in Randolph and Guilford counties, North Carolina. The plain-woven patterns are usually plaids or stripes of rich colors. These coverlets are made of two panels sewn together; the top and bottom are hemmed and the sides are selvage. Although the makers remain anonymous, these coverlets probably were woven in the Quaker or Scots-Irish communities in that area.

13. WOVEN COVERLET (DETAIL), *Randolph County, North Carolina, 1825–1860.*
Cotton and wool; 91" x 72 ¹/₂". *Acc. 3121.2.*

40

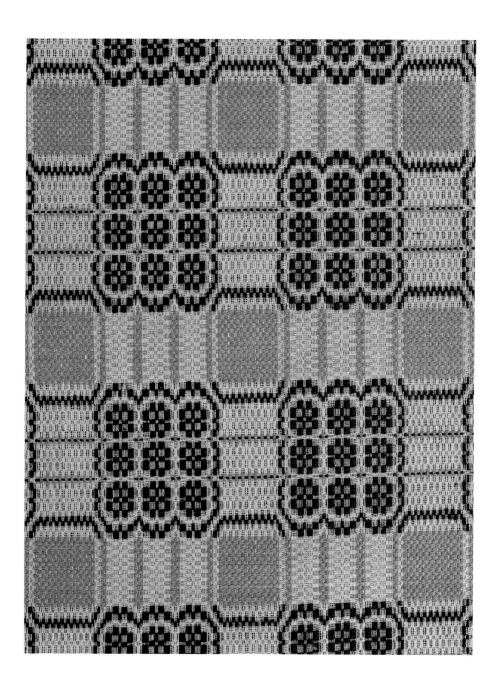

This coverlet, which descended in a family from the
Manchester area of Coffee County, is woven in a
variation of the Snowball pattern, also called the Rose
pattern. It is made of three widths sewn together. The top
and bottom are hemmed, and the sides are selvage.

15. OVERSHOT COVERLET (DETAIL), *attributed to Maryland, c. 1850.*
Cotton warp and weft with supplemental wool weft; 91" x 73". *Acc. 3011.2.*

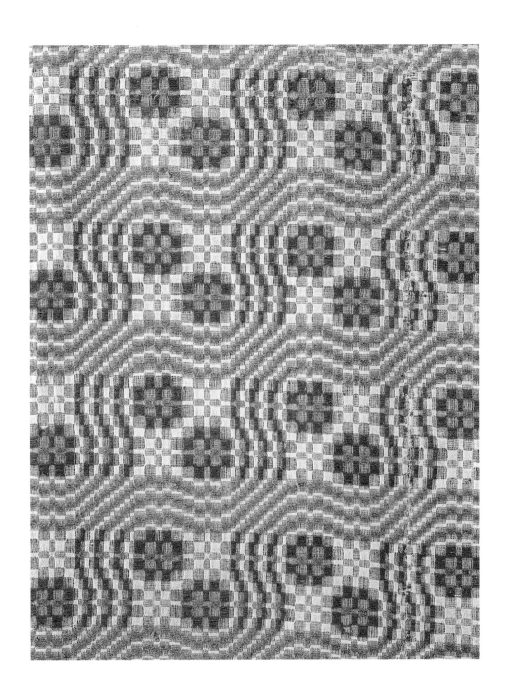

This coverlet, woven in the Snail's Trail pattern,
consists of three widths sewn together. The top and
bottom are hemmed, and the sides are selvage.

16. OVERSHOT COVERLET (DETAIL), *woven by Mary Emily Motsinger Raper (4 March 1834–15 November 1896), Arcadia, North Carolina, 1850–1860.*
Cotton warp and weft and supplemental wool weft; 90 ¾" x 68". *Acc. 4188.2.*

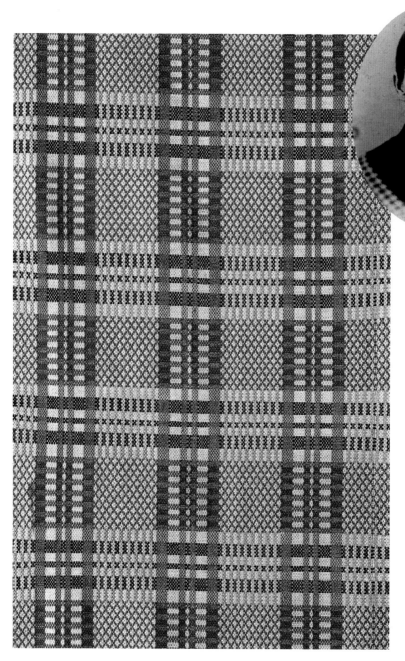

16a. PHOTOGRAPH OF MARY EMILY MOTSINGER RAPER *c. 1875, by Farrell & Stone photographers, Winston, North Carolina. Acc. 4188.3.*

This coverlet is woven in the Dog-Track pattern with a Diamond Table variation. One of a pair woven by Mary Emily Motsinger Raper, it consists of two panels sewn together. Mary Emily Motsinger married William Davis Raper on 28 April 1853. He later served in the Confederate Army. At the time of her death, each of her seven children received one of her prized possessions; this pair of coverlets came to MESDA through one of her descendants. Mary Emily and William Raper are buried in Arcadia at the Mount Olivet Methodist Church.

17. PIECED CHILD'S QUILT, *made by Harriet Kirk Marion (1782–1856),*
Belle Isle Plantation, St. John's, Berkeley County, South Carolina, 1830.
Cotton with linen back; 57 ⁵/₈" x 44". *Acc. 2534.1.*

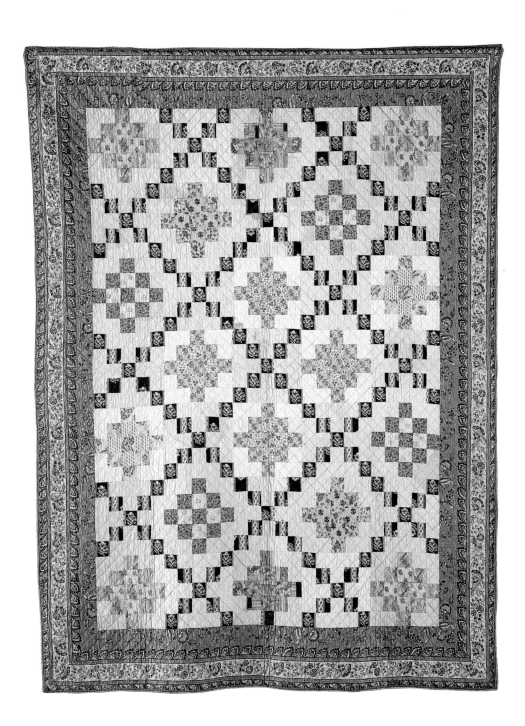

This pieced quilt is a variation on the Irish Chain pattern.
Its chintz border with mitered corners still retains its
glaze. There is no batting. It is quilted with diagonal lines
overall. Written in pencil on a cloth label sewn to the back
of the quilt is: "Quilt made by / Harriet Kirk Marion for
her granddaughter Harriet Marion Palmer / 1830 St. Johns
Berkley."

18. PIECED QUILT, *made by Harriet Kirk Marion (1782–1856), Belle Isle Plantation, St. John's, Berkeley County, South Carolina, 1840. Cotton with cotton back; 97 ¾" x 92 ¾". Acc. 2534.4.*

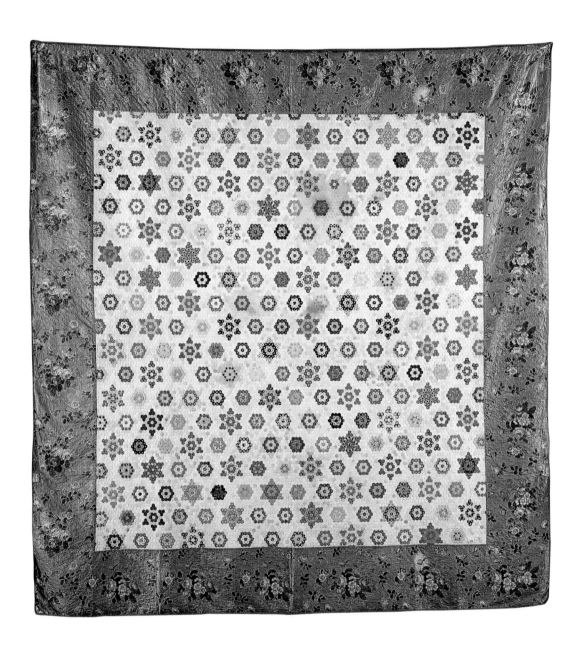

44

A wide border of glazed chintz with mitered corners surrounds the pieced top of small hexagonal patches in a honeycomb pattern. There is no batting. The pieced portion is cross-hatch quilted; while the border is marked for cross-hatch quilting, it is only parallel quilted. A new braid binds the edges. Written in ink on the reverse is "John G. Palmer / from his Grandmother / Mother." In pencil on a cloth label sewn to the back is: "Quilt made / by Harriet Kirk Marion / of St. Johns Berkley S.C. / for her grand son / John Gedron Palmer / 1840 / Marked by / Kate Palmer Logare / great granddaughter." This suggests that it was not quilted until a later date. A similar quilt in a private collection has been recorded by MESDA; it was made by Laura R. Dwight of Orangeburg, South Carolina, who also signed one of the blocks in cat. 20.

19. APPLIQUÉD QUILT, *made by Catherine Couturier Marion Palmer (1807–1895),*
St. John's, Berkeley County, South Carolina, 1847.
Cotton with cotton back and batting; 109 $^7/_8$" x 103 $^1/_4$". *Acc. 2534.2.*

This quilt has a double border of two strips of chintz alternating with one of plain cotton. The strips of each side of the border are of single pieces of fabric, and the corners are mitered. The center is worked in an appliquéd flowering tree pattern. The background of the center and the white border are cross-hatch quilted, and the chintz borders are quilted in diagonal parallel lines. On the back is written in ink: "Harriet M. Palmer from her mother." On a cloth label sewn to the back is written in pencil, "Quilt made by Catherine Couturier Marion Palmer Dwight St. John Berkeley SC. 1847."

20. PIECED AND APPLIQUÉD QUILT, *attributed to Catherine Couturier Marion Palmer (1807–1895),*
St. John's, Berkeley County, South Carolina, 1847–1848.
Cotton with cotton back and batting; 106" x 107 ½". *Acc. 2534.3.*

According to family tradition, Catherine Couturier Marion Palmer, together with other family members and friends, made this friendship quilt in the album style for her daughter Harriet Marion Palmer (born 1830), who married Francis Marion Dwight in 1850. It may have been made in anticipation of Harriet's marriage. The quilt consists of twenty-five blocks, each with a chintz design appliquéd to a white ground. The blocks are separated by bands of cotton print fabric. The overall quilting pattern is diamond cross-hatching except for the border, which is quilted in diagonal parallel lines. The glazed border has mitered corners. Some marking lines for the quilting pattern are still visible.

Many of the women who signed the blocks in cat. 20 are in some way related to the recipient. The blocks are inscribed with ink from left to right as follows:

Top row: *Eliza Catherine Palmer / Charleston / 1847; Caroline Felder / Sumter Ville / 1847; Martha Elizabeth Bonneau / Pineville 1847; Laura R. Dwight / Orangeburg / August 1847; Mrs. Lavinia Jamison / Orangeburg / 1847*

Second row: *1st block — no signature; Ann A. King / Sumter District/ 1848; M. V. Yeadon / Charleston / 1848; Mrs Harriet Marion / Mt. Pleasant / April 1847; M. A. Dwight / Orangeburg / August 10, 1847*

Third row: *M. A. Dingle / Oct. 14, 1847; Elizabeth Russell / Charleston / 1847; E. Russell / Charleston / 1847; Mary Elizabeth McKelvey / Mount Pleasant / 1847; Sarah Martha Kirk / Loch Dhu / 1847*

Fourth row: *Louisa C. King / Sumter / 1847; Elizabeth Russell / Charleston / 1847; Elizabeth Russell / Charleston / 1847; Mrs. Sophia Glover / Orangeburg / July 1847; Mrs. Carolina Gramblin / Orangeburg / 1847*

Bottom row: *F. A. Dwight / Orangeburg / August 10th 1847; Anna Adela McKelvey / Fountain Head / December 1847; Mary Rebecca Couturier / St. Johns Berkeley / 1847; Mary Yeadon / Charleston / 1847; Martha Bonneau / Pineville/ 1847*

REF: A similar friendship quilt, signed by H. Marion and M. V. Yeadon, among others, is illustrated in Christie's January 1992 auction catalogue, *Important American Furniture, Silver, Prints, Folk Art and Decorative Arts* (New York: Christie's, 1992), 164.

20a. Portrait of the Yeadon Family (detail), *1848, artist unknown.* Private collection.

Mary Videau Marion Yeadon and her adopted daughter Eliza Catherine Palmer each made and signed a square in the quilt shown as cat. 20. Mary Videau was the daughter of Harriet Kirk Marion and the sister of Catherine Couturier Marion Palmer, who assembled the quilt. Eliza Catherine was Catherine Palmer's daughter; her aunt and her aunt's husband, Richard Yeadon, adopted her after her father died.

REF: Christine Z. Fant, Margaret B. Hollis, and Virginia G. Meynard, eds., *South Carolina Portraits: A Collection of Portraits of South Carolinians and Portraits in South Carolina* (Columbia: National Society of the Colonial Dames of America in South Carolina, 1996), 425.

47

21. APPLIQUÉD AND PIECED COVERLET, *said to have been made by Sarah Willis Hayes,*
Gloucester County, Virginia, and Warren County, North Carolina, 1780–1810.
Cotton and linen with silk appliqué thread; 91 ³/₈" x 85". *Acc. 2669.*

48

Sarah Willis Hayes may have started this coverlet in
Gloucester County, Virginia, before moving to Warren
County, North Carolina. The multicolored fabrics are
woodblock-printed, the blue and red flower and bird
appliqués are of copperplate-printed fabric, and the
ground is plain cotton. The cut-out chintz appliqué is
applied with buttonhole and reverse buttonhole stitches in
silk thread to cover the raw cut edges, which are not fold-
ed under. The side strips of the border run the full length

of the sides; the corners are not mitered. It is not quilted,
and the backing is modern. The diamond-in-a-square center motif is similar to others from the lower Chesapeake.

REF: Gloria Seaman Allen, *First Flowerings: Early*
Virginia Quilts (Washington, D.C.: DAR Museum, 1987),
16; Bivins and Alexander, *Regional Arts of the Early*
South, 44.

22. APPLIQUÉD QUILT, *said to have been made by Elizabeth Gramby, Hertford,*
Perquimmans County, North Carolina, c. 1800.
Cotton with cotton back and batting; 91 ¹/₈" to 93 ¹/₄" x 90 ³/₈". *Acc. 2636.*

This quilt's diamond-in-a-square design is made of pieced chintz strips of roller-printed cotton. The center design of birds and foliage is made of cut-out chintz appliqué using woodblock-printed cotton fabric; the same motifs are repeated in the triangles surrounding the center diamond. The quilt has an appliquéd border of swags of the same roller-printed fabric as the square and diamond strips. The ground within the diamond and the square is quilted in a clamshell pattern, and the ground for the swag border is parallel quilted. The square and diamond borders are herringbone quilted. The central motif is appliquéd in cotton thread with a reverse buttonhole stitch.

23. APPLIQUÉD QUILT, *Piedmont North Carolina, c. 1820.*
Cotton with cotton back and batting; 101" x 100 ³/₈". *Acc. 2024.122.*

The Princess Feathers design of this quilt has appliqués in red-and-yellow print calico on a white ground. Its primary features are a central sixteen-pointed star with eight plumes emanating from it in the same fabric and a thistle in each corner. Reverse appliqué is effectively used in the thistles and the center star. Feather quilting outlines the appliqués, and the central design is encircled with feather quilting as well. The appliqués are applied with buttonhole stitches and are quilted. The border is a wood-block-printed fabric with mitered corners; it has a narrow white cotton binding.

Quilts, Coverlets & Counterpanes

24. APPLIQUÉD QUILT, *attributed to western Maryland, c. 1825.*
Cotton with cotton back and batting; 79 ¹/₂" x 89 ³/₄". *Acc. 3511.*

This quilt has a patriotic motif of an eagle with a shield body, holding a leafy branch in its beak, surrounded with ten stars, rather than the usual thirteen. The eagle is centered from top to bottom but not side to side. The rest of the quilt top is decorated with a lively design of individual flowers, bouquets, circles, stars, vines, and leaves. The imaginative use of appliqué, reverse appliqué, applied cording, channel quilting, and decorative quilting patterns enhances the visual effect.

25. APPLIQUÉD AND PIECED QUILT, *made by Mrs. William Taylor, Savannah, Georgia, 1832.* Cotton with cotton back and batting; 99" x 106". *Acc. 3064.2.*

The cross-stitched dedication, in blue thread, "A C Taylor / from his / Grand Mother / 1832," appears below the center appliqué. The appliquéd fruit, baskets, birds, flowers, and cherubs of this quilt are cut from printed chintz and applied with a reverse buttonhole stitch in silk thread. Some decorative surface embroidery accents the fabric patterns. The zig-zag border was assembled as pieced strips; it is surrounded by a border of a strip of white and a strip of printed fabric. The central panel is double-row quilted in a cross-hatched pattern, and the borders have straight parallel quilting with some herringbone quilting. The backing is a small brown floral print cotton. Mrs. Taylor was the daughter of Elizabeth Clount Miller and Andrew Miller of North Carolina. She made another quilt now in the MESDA collection; it has a central medallion with birds in a flowering tree motif and is inscribed "Alex.dr M. Taylor. July 1803."

Quilts, Coverlets & Counterpanes

26. Appliquéd and pieced quilt, *attributed to North Carolina, c. 1850.*
Cotton with cotton back and batting; 79 ¼" x 78 ½". *Acc. 1166.*

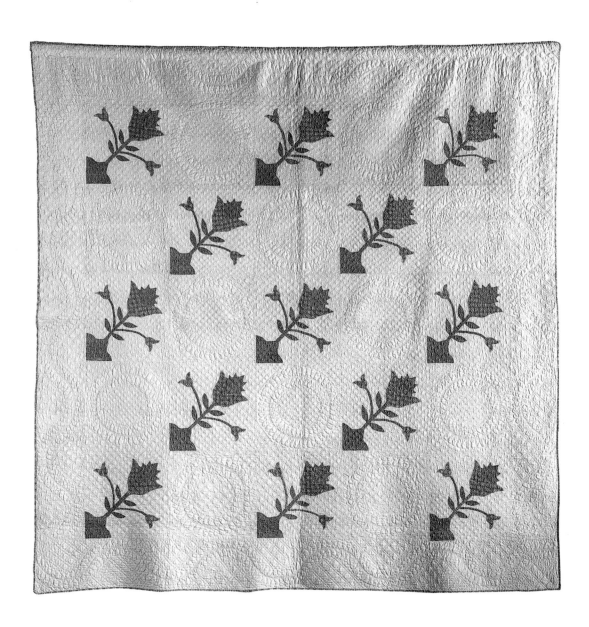

This quilt in the North Carolina Lily pattern consists of twenty-five white cotton squares. Every other square has an appliquéd lily in red and green calico, all facing the same direction. The background of these squares is quilted in double cross-hatching, and the solid white squares are quilted in a detailed circle pattern filled in with double cross-hatching. The border is quilted in an undulating feather motif with double cross-hatching. The quilt is *bound in the same red fabric used in the lilies. Quilts with green and red printed textiles on elaborately quilted white backgrounds were especially popular in mid-nineteenth century America.*

Ref: *Two Hundred Years of the Visual Arts in North Carolina* (Raleigh: North Carolina Museum of Art, 1976), 130.

27. APPLIQUÉD QUILT, *made by Mary Guyton, Baltimore, Maryland, c. 1850.*
Cotton with cotton back and batting; 93 ³/₄" x 94". *Acc. 3678.*

This album quilt is made of twenty-five appliquéd squares, decorated with a small amount of chain-stitch embroidery. There is a symmetry and balance to the arrangement of the blocks. The red and green fabrics used were popular in the mid-nineteenth century. It is quilted all over, except in the appliquéd areas, in a double-row herringbone pattern. The sawtooth border is a green cotton fabric with brown speckles. Cross-stitched on the top center of the back are the initials "MG." On a more modern cotton label sewn to the back is written: "Album Pieced and Quilted / by Mary Guyton-Beatty. before 1853. Great-grandmother of Helen Margaret Beatty. / Goes to Helen Margaret Beatty."

28. PIECED AND APPLIQUÉD QUILT, *made by Alice Baynes, Baltimore, Maryland, c. 1850.* Cotton with cotton back and batting; 104" x 99 ¹/₂". *Acc. 3011.1.*

This quilt, with the initials "AB" in one corner, has been extensively repaired in the twentieth century, with some of the fabrics replaced, some areas requilted, and some machine-stitching repairs. The thirteen decorated blocks are pieced together by strips of fabric forming a diagonal grid, surrounded by half and quarter blocks. The symbolism of the two houses under the willow tree in the center panel and the pieces of a house on opposite sides of the quilt, combined with the use of exuberantly decorated hearts, suggests that this was a wedding quilt. The borders are pieced and cross-hatch and herringbone quilted. The thirteen blocks are parallel quilted with some outline quilting.

29. APPLIQUÉD QUILT, *made by Maria Lavinia Vogler, Salem, North Carolina, c. 1853.* Cotton with cotton back and batting; 90 ½" x 74". *Acc. 4173.5.*

56

This is one of the few quilts known to have been made in Salem. It is made of thirty squares sewn together, with every other square appliquéd in the Rose pattern and the background quilted in diagonal parallel lines. The white squares are quilted in a six-pointed compass flower enclosed by a circle, from which radiate pointed oval leaves in a wreath design. The border is made up of three strips of the same fabric used in the appliqué. A note attached to the back of this quilt says: "Old quilt made by Lavenia Vogler about 1852 or 1853. Mama Rosa wants

'Peggy' L. to have it when she dies (or Margaret). Nov 11 - 1932 — Dora & I packing quilts after the aux. Showing 1936." Another note attached to the quilt says: "Made by Lavenia Vogler about 1853. Loaned by her daughter Rosa M. Fries." Maria Lavinia Vogler (25 December 1833–18 May 1896) was the daughter of the Salem gunsmith Timothy Vogler and his wife Charlotte Hamilton Vogler. She married Salem tinsmith Julius Mickey on 28 September 1857. They had one child, Rosa Elvira (24 May 1860 – 6 August 1938), who married her second cousin Henry Elias Fries (son of Lisetta and Francis Fries) on 20 April 1881.

29a. PHOTOGRAPH OF THE TIMOTHY VOGLER FAMILY, 1895. *Private collection.*

This shows (in the back row) Maria Lavinia Vogler Mickey (fourth from left), her husband Julius Mickey to her right, and Rosa Mickey, far right.

30. PIECED QUILT, *American, late eighteenth or early nineteenth century.*
Cotton, linen, and wool top with wool filling and back; 79" x 65 ½". *Acc. 476.78.*

58

This quilt top is an arrangement of geometric shapes cut from linen, cotton, and wool fabrics. The frame around the central eight-pointed star is quilted in an undulating line, and the four corners of the next border are quilted in a stylized six-petaled flower. The outermost border, which is made of various lengths of fabric, is quilted in an undulating vine-and-leaf pattern. This quilt is an excellent example of the use of scraps of available fabric.

31. PIECED QUILT, *made by "EW," Jarrettsville, Maryland, 1796.*
Cotton with cotton back and batting; 88 ³/₄" x 85 ³/₄". *Acc. 3271.*

This quilt is cross-stitched on the back "E*W 1*7*96."
"EW" is thought to be a member of the Webster family of
Jarrettsville, Maryland, possibly Elizabeth Webster. This
quilt top has thirteen different woodblock-printed cotton
fabrics. The patches were sewn together in a pattern that
uses the variety of fabrics to best advantage. Eighteenth-
century pieced quilts in a framed center style are rare.

REF: Gloria Seaman Allen, "Bedcoverings, Kent County,
Maryland, 1710–1820," *Uncoverings 1985* (Research
Papers of the American Quilt Study Group), vol. 6, 25;
Colleen R. Callahan, "A Quilt and Its Pieces,"
Metropolitan Museum Journal 19/20 (1986), 106–7.

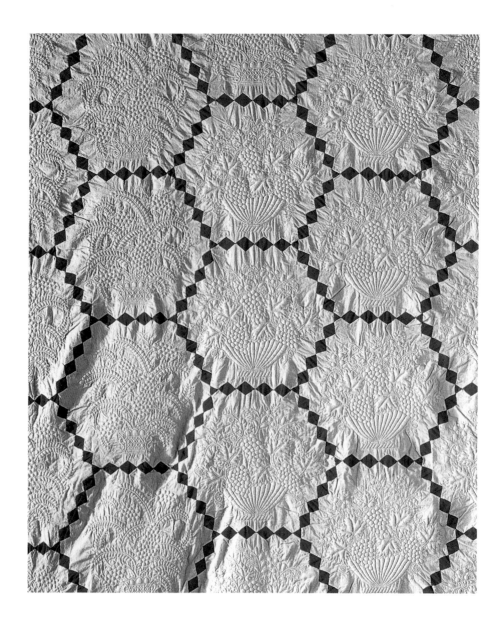

Fifty-two complete stuffed-work hexagons and twenty-three partial hexagons along the edges, bordered by bold red diamonds, make up this unfinished coverlet. Each hexagon is worked in one of two intricate floral motifs. The backing was quilted to the top fabric and stuffed, *after which any excess backing was cut away close to the quilting lines. Because it is unfinished, the quilt top shows signs of the steps used in its production: some basting stitches and the paper templates for the diamonds are still in place along one side.*

Quilts, Coverlets & Counterpanes

33. PIECED STRIP QUILT, *made by Elizabeth "Bess" Abrams Renwick,*
Newberry County, South Carolina, c. 1840.
Silk with cotton back and batting; 84 ¼" x 87". *Acc. 4094.*

In 1807, over thirty years before she made this quilt, Bess Abrams Renwick (1782–1863) made the counterpane shown as cat. 6. In 1810 she married William Renwick, who died in 1816, at which time she seems to have taken over the management of their farm. She completed this quilt about 1840. This quilt uses three silk fabrics that have been cut into strips and sewn together. The strips are 2 ¾" to 3 ⅜" wide. The quilting pattern is a variation of cross-hatching. The edge binding is also silk, blue on right and left and brown on top and bottom.

34. Pieced and embroidered quilt, *made by Mary Redman Parrish, Cynthiana, Kentucky, 1865–1875.*
Silk and wool with wool embroidery thread, cotton batting, and backing of rose-colored wool.
The center has a white cotton foundation and the border has a brown cotton inner lining; 90" x 89".
Acc. 2726.

Mary "Molly" Redman was born on 7 June 1847 and died on the dining room table in her home in Cynthiana on 19 August 1904 while undergoing surgery for a malignancy. She was the wife of W. A. Parrish (1845–1893); they had four children. This Honeycomb quilt is made up of many small silk and wool hexagons which are pieced together to make larger hexagons; the border is of silk embroidered with a floral design in wool. From the back, the cross-hatch quilting is apparent. A portrait of Mary Redman appears as cat. 34a.

34a. PORTRAIT OF MARY REDMAN AS A CHILD,
c. 1850. Artist unknown.
Private collection.

34b. UNFINISHED HEXAGON SECTIONS
FOR A QUILT TOP, *Salem, North Carolina.*
Silk and paper. *Acc. 4355.1–18.*

*The note that accompanies these sections states,
"Pieced by two little girls — ages 8 & 10 yrs. old —
my grandmother & her sister [Martha Wilson and Mary
Wilson Welfare]. Because their little hands couldn't hold
the big scissors, all these pieces were cut out with candle
snuffers. Circa 1848–1850." The explanation about
candle snuffers is faulty, but the paper templates and
basting stitches demonstrate the steps involved in piecing
such a quilt. Someone had begun to assemble the
hexagon patches with borders of small black hexagons.*

35. Pieced quilt, *made by Lisetta Maria Vogler Fries, Salem, North Carolina, 1873.*
Cotton with cotton back and batting; 88 ³/₄" x 73". *Acc. Q-111.*

This quilt is a variation of the Washington Sidewalk, with quotations written in ink. They include verses from the Old and New Testaments and quotations from the works of William Cowper, Edward Young, William Shakespeare, Alexander Pope, Walter Scott, John Milton, and Count

Nicholas Zinzendorf, the eighteenth-century leader of the Unitas Fratrum (Moravians), among others. A quote from Pope's "Essay on Man" illustrates the common theme: "Honor and shame from no condition rise / Act well your part — there all / the honour lies."

Lisetta Vogler Fries (3 March 1820–23 October 1903)
was the daughter of Salem silversmith John Vogler and his
wife Christina Spach Vogler. She was one of three children.
In 1838 she married Francis Fries, and they had seven
children. Cat. 35 is one of three similar quilts that she is
said to have made. Family tradition says that Lisetta made
this quilt for her daughter Mary Fries (31 August 1844–21
October 1927), who had married Rufus Patterson on 14
June 1864. The middle block of the bottom row is
inscribed in ink, "Mary Fries Patterson. / August 31st
1873." This would have been her twenty-ninth birthday.

35b. PHOTOGRAPH OF MARY FRIES, *c. 1860, taken*
in Florence, Italy, while on a trip to Europe.
Acc. 4241.162.

65

35a. PORTRAIT OF LISETTA MARIA VOGLER FRIES
AND HER HUSBAND FRANCIS FRIES
by Gustavus Grunewald, Salem,
North Carolina, 1839.
Oil on canvas; 12" x 10". *Acc. 2343.*

36. FOUNDATION-PIECED PATCHWORK QUILT, *American, 1860–1880.*
Silk, cotton, and wool with a solid brown cotton back and a cotton foundation; 78" x 63". *Acc. 3518.1.*

This pieced quilt was made in the Courtyard Steps variation of the Log Cabin design. It is representative of a type of quilt that was first developed during the years of the Lincoln presidency. This example shows a rather random arrangement of colors. Each square is 6 3/4" x 6 3/4".

Quilts, Coverlets & Counterpanes

37. PIECED QUILT, *attributed to Salem or Winston, North Carolina, 1880–1900.*
Silk with cotton twill back and cotton batting; 79" x 70 ½". *Acc. 4029.1.*

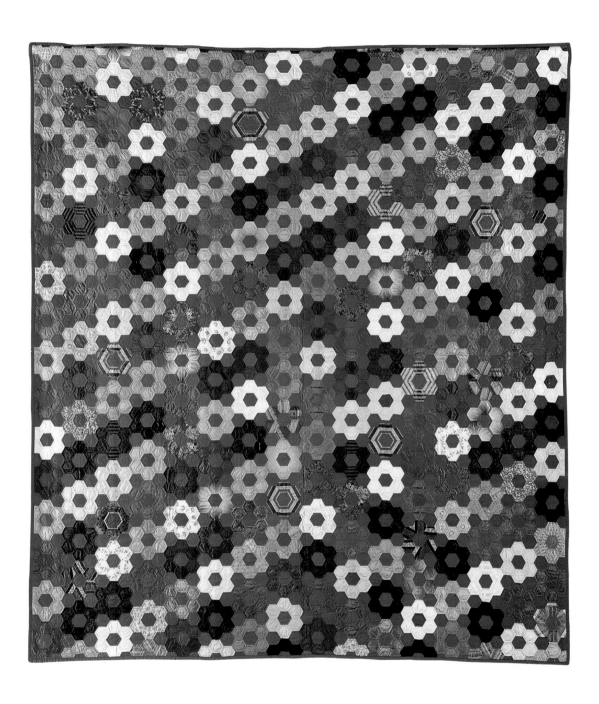

This silk quilt is the Grandmother's Flower Garden pattern. It is made of hexagons pieced in a flower design and channel quilted. The binding of red silk is machine sewn, and the backing is a brown cotton twill. The small size of this piece indicates that it could have been a "slumber throw," which was fashionable at this time.

38. FOUNDATION-PIECED CRAZY QUILT, *attributed to Salem or Winston, North Carolina, 1880–1900.* Silk velvet with silk embroidery and binding, with cotton twill back; 74" x 76 $^{5}/_{8}$". *Acc. Q-105.*

This quilt is made of twenty blocks, each made of irregular-shaped patches, with a solid border on two opposite sides. The patches are sewn together with a variety of decorative stitches in silk. Velvets used include solid colors, *ribs, prints, and stripes. Some patches are embroidered in silk or silk chenille, and some are appliquéd in silk or silk ribbon.*

The popular embroidered motifs used in this quilt include butterflies, a fan, a teacup and saucer, a bird in flight, a cat, an owl sitting in a crescent moon, and numerous identifiable flowers such as lily of the valley, pansies, bleeding hearts, and roses. The silk binding is machine stitched. The backing is a brownish purple cotton twill which is randomly tied.

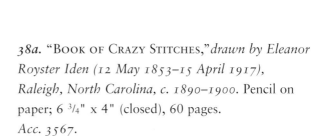

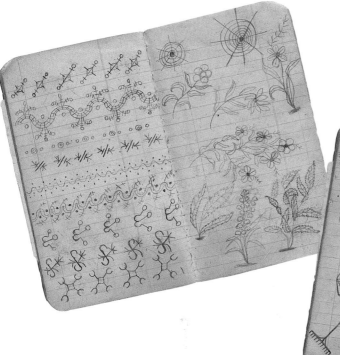

Crazy quilts were popular in the late Victorian period. The elaborate stitches used were an integral part of the design, and some seamstresses made sample books of stitches, such as the one shown here, which was assembled by Eleanor Royster Iden of Raleigh, North Carolina. Eleanor was the daughter of David Royster, a cabinetmaker in Raleigh, and his wife Sarah Womble. Some of the popular motifs from cat. 38, such as a butterfly, fans, and the lily of the valley, appear in this sample book as well.

38a. "BOOK OF CRAZY STITCHES," *drawn by Eleanor Royster Iden (12 May 1853–15 April 1917), Raleigh, North Carolina, c. 1890–1900. Pencil on* paper; 6 ³/₄" x 4" (closed), 60 pages. *Acc. 3567.*

39. PIECED DOLL QUILT, *attributed to Salem, North Carolina, late nineteenth century.*
Cotton with cotton back and batting; 17 ⁷/₈" x 13 ³/₄". *Acc. Q-101.*

70

This doll-sized quilt is made of twelve blocks. Six blocks
are in a variation of a simple eight-pointed star, and six
are made of one piece of cotton. The patches vary in size.
The back is one piece of brown and blue plaid cotton,
which folds around to the front to create the binding.

Bibliography

Allen, Gloria Seaman. "Bedcoverings, Kent County, Maryland, 1710–1820." *Uncoverings 1985* (Research Papers of the American Quilt Study Group, vol. 6), 9–31.

———. *First Flowerings: Early Virginia Quilts.* Washington, D.C.: DAR Museum, 1987.

———. *Old Line Traditions: Maryland Women and Their Quilts.* Washington, D.C.: DAR Museum, 1985.

Bed Ruggs / 1722–1833 (exhibition catalogue). Hartford, Conn.: Wadsworth Atheneum, 1972.

Bivins, John, and Forsyth Alexander, *The Regional Arts of the Early South* (Winston-Salem, N.C.: MESDA, 1991).

Blum, Dilys, and Jack L. Lindsey. "Nineteenth-Century Appliqué Quilts." *Philadelphia Museum of Art Bulletin,* fall 1989.

Brackman, Barbara. *Clues in the Calico: A Guide to Identifying and Dating Antique Quilts.* McLean, Va.: EPM Publications, 1989.

———. "A Chronological Index to Pieced Quilt Patterns, 1775–1825." *Uncoverings 1983* (Research Papers of the American Quilt Study Group, vol. 4), 99–127.

Bullard, Lacy Folmar, and Betty Jo Shiell. *Chintz Quilts: Unfading Glory.* Tallahassee, Fla.: Serendipity Publishers, 1983.

Callahan, Colleen R. "A Quilt and Its Pieces." *Metropolitan Museum Journal* 19/20 (1986), 97–141.

Cooper, Grace Rogers. *The Copp Family Textiles.* Washington, D.C.: Smithsonian Institution Press, 1971.

Frost, S. Annie. *The Ladies' Guide to Needle Work, Embroidery, Etc.: Being a Complete Guide to All Kinds of Ladies' Fancy Work.* New York, 1877; reprint, Mendocino, Calif.: R. L. Shep, 1986.

Hargrove, John. *The Weavers Draft Book and Clothiers Assistant.* Introduction by Rita J. Adrosko. Worcester, Mass.: American Antiquarian Society, 1979.

Horton, Laurel. "The Textile Industry and South Carolina Quilts." *Uncoverings 1988* (Research Papers of the American Quilt Study Group, vol. 9), 129–50.

Horton, Laurel. "Quiltmaking Traditions in South Carolina." *Uncoverings 1984* (Research Papers of the American Quilt Study Group, vol. 5), 55–69.

Katzenberg, Dena. *Baltimore Album Quilts.* Baltimore, Md.: Baltimore Museum of Art, 1981.

McKendry, Ruth. *Quilts and Other Bed Coverings in the Canadian Tradition.* Toronto: Van Nostrand Reinhold, 1979.

Michie, Audrey. "Charleston Textile Imports, 1738–1742." *Journal of Early Southern Decorative Arts* VII, 1 (1981), 21–39.

Montgomery, Florence M. *Textiles in America 1650–1870.* A Winterthur Book. New York: W. W. Norton & Company, 1984.

———. *Printed Textiles in America 1650–1870.* A Winterthur Book. New York: W. W. Norton & Company, 1970.

Museum of Early Southern Decorative Arts. *Guide to the Index of Early Southern Artists and Artisans.* New York: Clearwater Publishing Co., 1985. Microfiche.

Roberson, Ruth Haislip. *North Carolina Quilts.* Chapel Hill: University of North Carolina Press, 1988.

Rogers, Gay Ann. *An Illustrated History of Needleworking Tools.* London: John Murray, 1983.

Ramsey, Bets, and Merikay Waldvogel. *The Quilts of Tennessee: Images of Domestic Life Prior to 1930.* Nashville, Tenn.: Rutledge Hill Press, 1986.

Stone, Robert G., and David M. Hinkley, eds. *Clark's Other Journal: William and Julia H. Clark's Household and Homemaking Recipes, Home Remedies, and a Partial Inventory of the Families Personal Belongings as Recorded by William Clark —1820.* Lee's Summit, Mo.: Fat Little Pudding Boy's Press, 1995.

The Workwoman's Guide, Containing Instructions to the Inexperienced in Cutting Out and Completing Those Articles of Wearing Apparel, &c,. Which Are Usually Made at Home; Also, Explanations on Upholstery, Straw-Platting, Bonnet Making, Knitting, &c. By a Lady. London: Simpkin, Marshall, and Co., 1838.